Christmas Quilting

Edited by Jeanne Stauffer
and Sandra L. Hatch

HOUSE of
WHITE
BIRCHES

PUBLISHERS
SINCE 1947

Editors: Sandra L. Hatch, Jeanne Stauffer
Associate Editor: Barb Sprunger
Copy Editors: Cathy Reef, Mary Jo Kurten

Photography: Tammy Christian, Nancy Sharp
Photography Assistants: Linda Quinlan, Arlou Wittwer

Creative Coordinator: Shaun Venish
Production Coordinator: Brenda Gallmeyer
Traffic Coordinator: Sandra Beres
Technical Artist: Connie Rand
Production Assistants: Shirley Blalock, Carol Dailey
Book/Cover Design: Sandy Bauman

Publishers: Carl H. Muselman, Arthur K. Muselman
Chief Executive Officer: John Robinson
Marketing Director: Scott Moss
Editorial Director: Vivian Rothe
Production Director: George Hague

Printed in the United States of America
First Printing: 1999
Library of Congress Number: 99-94090
ISBN: 1-882138-45-7

Every effort has been made to ensure the accuracy and completeness of the instructions in this book. However, we cannot be responsible for human error, for the results when using materials other than those specified in the instructions or for variations in individual work.

Front cover: Christmas Star, page 126

I love the Christmas season. I try to make it last the whole year by constantly looking for gifts all year long. I look for bargains and sales and sometimes I have next year's gifts chosen before this year's gifts have been given. You know how it is when you find the perfect gift for a person—you just can't pass it up. I reserve several shelves of a storage closet for the gifts and sometimes I am organized enough to write down what I have and who it is for. This habit relieves much of the stress of last-minute shopping and trying to find the right thing when it isn't there.

Our gift to you this year is this wonderful book filled with projects that will make perfect gifts for almost anyone on your shopping list. You can still shop but in fabric stores and quilt shops—your favorite places!

There is nothing better than handmade gifts made with lots of love and precious time. Not only are they appreciated at the moment but many of them become heirlooms to be used for years and then passed on. A part of you is remembered each time they are displayed or used.

Take some time now to sit down and browse through this book. You will find projects for the beginner and the most experienced quilters. Some projects can be made in a day while others will take weeks, depending on your choice of construction.

Over 20 years ago my aunt made me a quilled tree ornament made from a goose egg. I have placed this ornament on my tree every Christmas since. After the holidays I carefully pack it in its own box so it won't get broken during storage. This year as I hung the ornament, tears came to my eyes. My aunt had died this past year. There is no chance that I will forget her during the holiday season. When I no longer need this ornament, one of my children will keep her memory alive every Christmas as well. I wonder if she ever realized how much of a memory she made when she gave me this ornament.

Have a wonderful time making heirlooms and memories and have a Merry Christmas.

Sandra L. Hatch

Contents

- Chapter 5 -
General Instructions

A Merry Little Christmas

Ornaments, tree skirts, garlands and candle mats! These may be little in size, but they're an important part of Christmas. In this chapter, you'll find over 20 projects to decorate your tree or to give as gifts to family and friends. We've included several small wall quilts, some that you can hang for Christmas and enjoy all winter long. A little quilting adds a lot of love to the Christmas season.

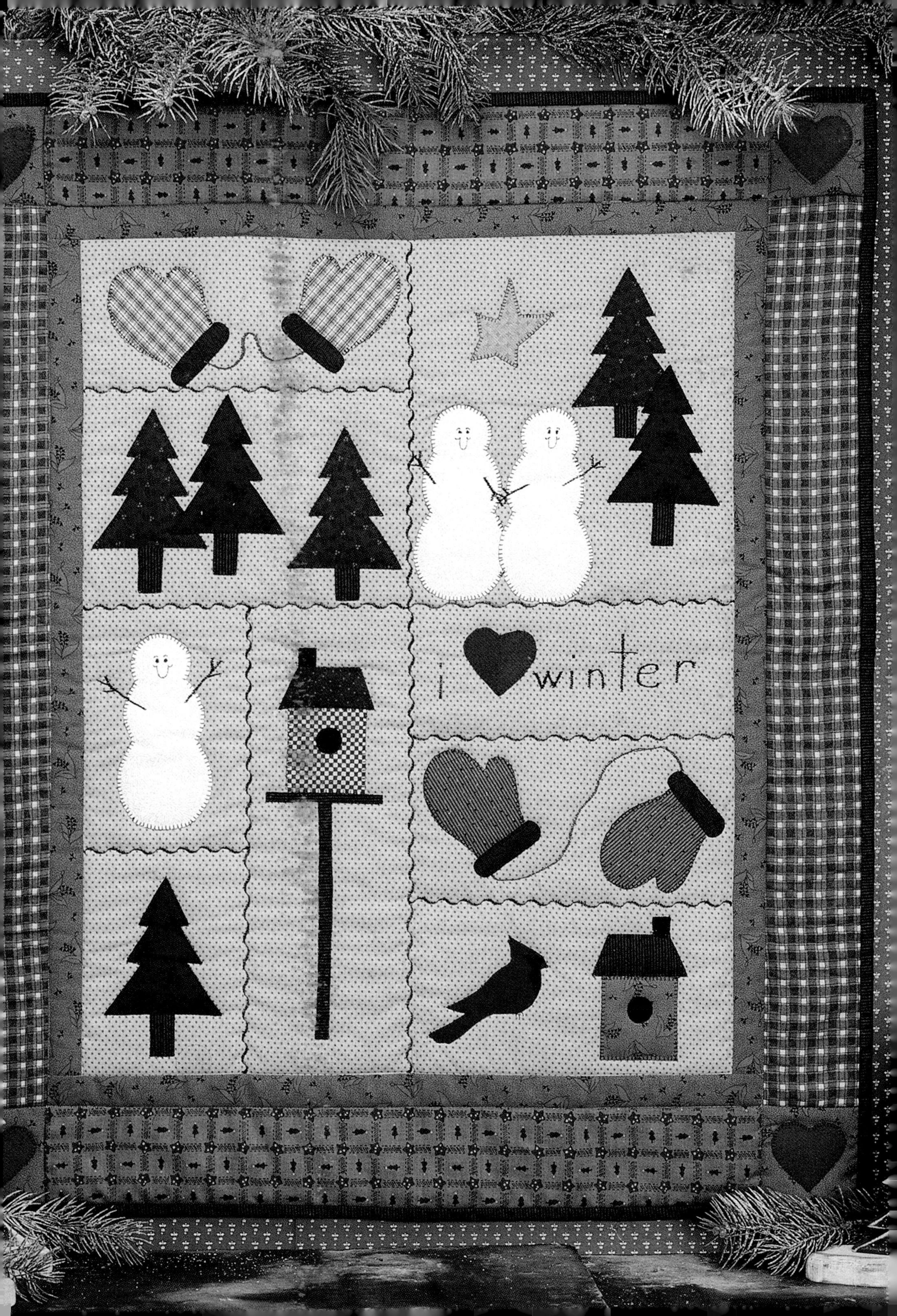
i winter

I Love Winter

By Meredith Yoder

I f you like the cold and snowy days of winter, make this wall quilt to share your love of the season with all who come to visit. The smiling snowmen will welcome everyone to your home.

- **Skill Level:** Intermediate
- **Project Size:** 29" x 34"

- 3" x 3" scrap each gold print and black solid
- 4" x 4" scrap navy print
- Fat eighth of each of the following: brown-and-black stripe; red, dark green 1, dark green 2, blue and white-on-white prints; blue plaid; and red check
- 1/4 yard of each of the following: blue check, medium green print and medium brown print
- 5/8 yard tan print
- Backing 33" x 38"
- Cotton batting 33" x 38"
- 4 yards self-made or purchased binding
- 1 spool each blue, black and off-white all-purpose thread
- 1 spool clear monofilament
- 3/4 yard fusible transfer web
- Basic sewing supplies and tools, water-soluble fabric marker, permanent black fabric pen, ruler and pencil

Instructions

Step 1. Cut a piece of tan print 21 1/2" x 26 1/2". Using a water-soluble fabric marker, divide into nine sections referring to Figure 1 for sizes.

Step 2. Cut two strips each medium brown print 1 1/2" x 26 1/2" and 1 1/2" x 23 1/2". Sew the longer strips to opposite long sides and the shorter strips to

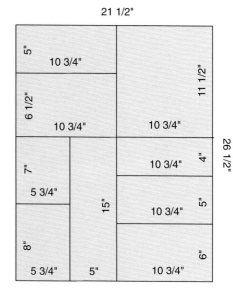

Figure 1
Divide background in sections as shown.

the top and bottom of the marked tan print background. Press seams toward strips.

Step 3. Cut two strips blue check 3 1/2" x 28 1/2"; sew to opposite long sides of pieced section. Press seams toward strips.

Step 4. Cut two strips medium green print 3 1/2" x 23 1/2" and four squares medium brown print 3 1/2" x 3 1/2". Sew a medium brown print square to each end of the medium green print strips; press seams toward strips. Sew a strip to the top and bottom of the pieced section; press seams toward strips.

Step 5. Prepare templates for each appliqué shape using pattern pieces given. Trace each shape as directed for number to cut onto the paper side of the fusible transfer web leaving a 1/2" margin around each piece. Cut out shapes in margins. Place shapes on the wrong side of fabrics as indicated on pattern for color; fuse in place. Cut out shapes on traced lines; remove paper backing.

Step 6. Referring to the Placement Diagram and photo of project, position pieces on background; fuse in place. Fuse hearts on border corner squares.

Step 7. Prepare top for quilting and finishing referring to General Instructions. ***Note:*** *Designer used brown-and-black stripe used for tree trunks for binding fabric.*

Step 8. Using black all-purpose thread in the top of the machine and off-white all-purpose thread in the bobbin, machine buttonhole-stitch or blanket-stitch around each shape. Using a medium-width zigzag stitch, add snowman branch arms. Using the same stitch and blue all-purpose thread in the top of the machine and off-white all-purpose thread in the bobbin, add strings connecting mittens in both mitten sections.

Step 9. Using permanent black fabric pen, add snowman faces referring to patterns.

Step 10. Mark words on heart section using water-soluble fabric marker. Stitch letters using a medium-width zigzag stitch using black all-purpose thread in the top of the machine and off-white all-purpose thread in the bobbin. Using the same threads and a machine scallop stitch, stitch lines dividing sections.

Step 11. Using clear nylon monofilament in the top of the machine and off-white all-purpose thread in the bobbin, machine-quilt in the ditch of border seams to finish. ●

I Love Winter
Placement Diagram
29" x 34"

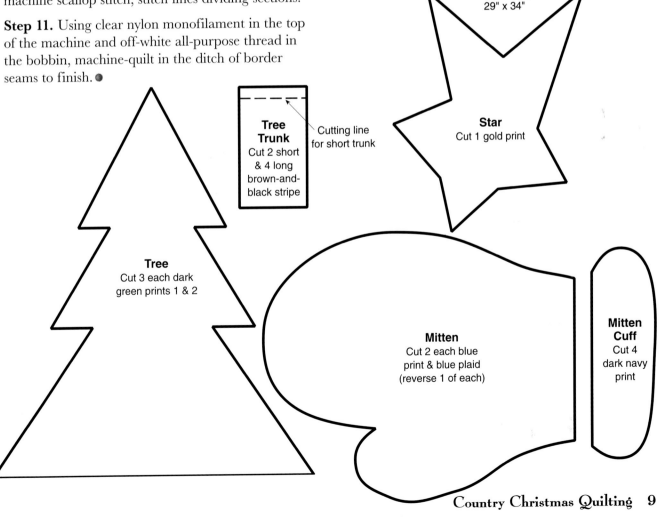

Tree Trunk
Cut 2 short & 4 long brown-and-black stripe

Cutting line for short trunk

Tree
Cut 3 each dark green prints 1 & 2

Star
Cut 1 gold print

Mitten
Cut 2 each blue print & blue plaid (reverse 1 of each)

Mitten Cuff
Cut 4 dark navy print

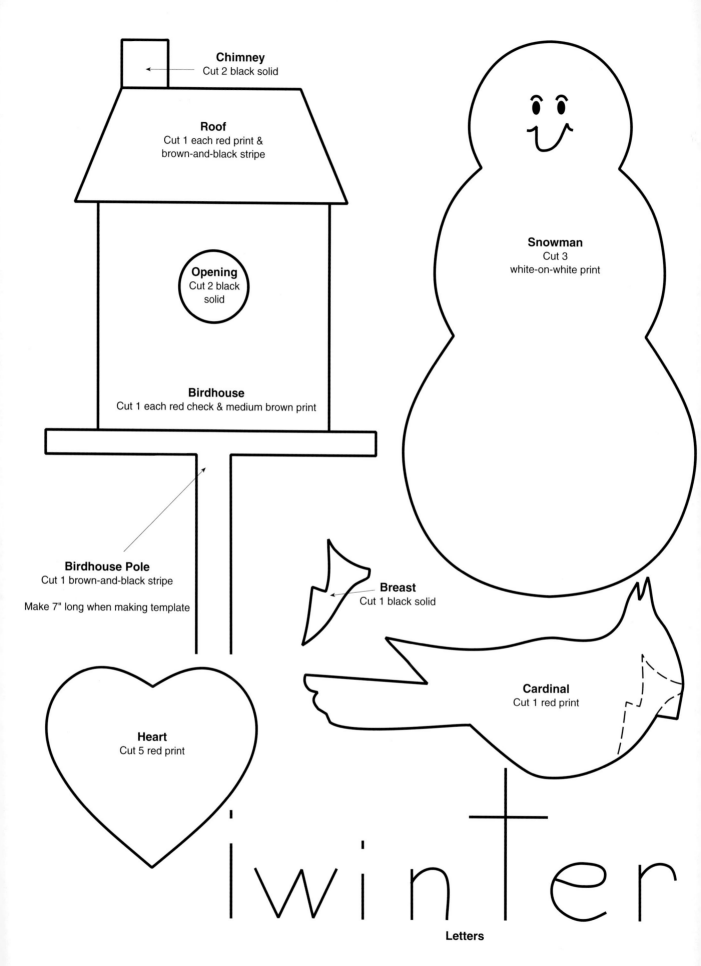

Chimney
Cut 2 black solid

Roof
Cut 1 each red print &
brown-and-black stripe

Opening
Cut 2 black
solid

Birdhouse
Cut 1 each red check & medium brown print

Birdhouse Pole
Cut 1 brown-and-black stripe

Make 7" long when making template

Heart
Cut 5 red print

Snowman
Cut 3
white-on-white print

Breast
Cut 1 black solid

Cardinal
Cut 1 red print

winter

Letters

Homecoming

By Christine Carlson

Small quilts are always a big hit during the holiday season. They require much less time to construct than larger quilts, and they fit in almost anywhere. Although this country-style mini looks complicated, it is easy and fun to make either for yourself or to give as a gift.

- **Skill Level:** Intermediate
- **Quilt Size:** 12 1/4" x 12 1/4"
- **Block Size:** 2 1/4" x 2 1/4"
- **Number of Blocks:** 9

- 5" x 8" piece medium blue print
- 11" x 18" piece white print
- 4" x 10" piece tan print
- 5" x 10" piece red print
- 2" x 9" piece dark green print
- 6" x 13" piece medium green print
- 2" x 6" piece dark brown print
- 11" x 18" piece medium brown print
- 2" x 4" piece black print
- 4" x 5" piece light pink print
- 8" x 10" piece medium pink print
- 10" x 13" piece green-and-white print
- Backing 16" x 16"
- Lightweight batting 16" x 16"
- Neutral color all-purpose thread
- White quilting thread
- 5 (5/8") star buttons
- Basic sewing supplies and tools and 45-degree-angle tool

Project Notes

Instructions are given for cutting pieces without templates. Quick-piecing instructions are given.

Use a fine machine needle No. 65 or 70 for all machine sewing.

Figure drawing arrows show direction to press seams.

Cutting

Step 1. Cut two A strips 1 1/8" x 5", one B strip 1" x 5", four C squares 1 1/2" x 1 1/2", one J strip 1 3/4" x 12" and two K strips 1 1/2" x 6" from 11" x 18" piece white print.

Step 2. Cut two D strips 3/4" x 5" and two E strips 1 1/8" x 8" from 5" x 8" piece medium blue print.

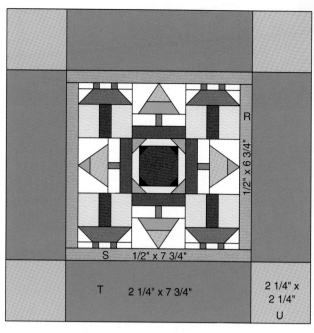

Homecoming
Placement Diagram
12 1/4" x 12 1/4"

Step 3. Cut two F strips 1 3/8" x 10" from 4" x 10" piece tan print.

Step 4. Cut one G strip 1" x 10" and one N square 2" x 2" from 5" x 10" piece red print.

Step 5. Cut one H strip 1" x 9" from 2" x 9" piece dark green print.

Step 6. Cut one I strip 1 1/4" x 9" and four U squares 2 3/4" x 2 3/4" from 6" x 13" piece medium green print.

Step 7. Cut one L strip 3/4" x 6" from 2" x 6" piece dark brown print.

Step 8. Cut one M strip 1" x 12" and five strips 1" x 11" for binding from 11" x 18" piece medium brown print.

Step 9. Cut two O squares 1 3/8" x 1 3/8" from 2" x 4" piece black print.

Step 10. Cut two P strips 7/8" x 2" and two P1 strips 7/8" x 2 3/4" from 4" x 5" piece light pink print.

Step 11. Cut two Q squares 1 5/8" x 1 5/8", two R strips 1" x 7 1/4" and two S strips 1" x 8 1/4" from 8" x 10" piece medium pink print.

Step 12. Cut four T strips 2 3/4" x 8 1/4" from 10" x 13" piece green-and-white print.

Piecing House Blocks

Step 1. Sew all 5"-long strips together to make A-D-

B-D-A strip set as shown in Figure 1; press seams open and trim to 1/8". Cut four 3/4"-wide segments from strip set to make chimney sections.

Step 2. Cut two 3 1/2"-long segments from each E strip. Using a 45-degree-angle tool, cut each E segment at a 45-degree angle on both ends, measuring in 1 1/8" from edge as shown in Figure 2.

Step 3. Cut C squares in half on one diagonal to make eight C triangles.

Step 4. Sew a C triangle to each angled side of E to make C-E-C roof section as shown in Figure 3; repeat for four sections.

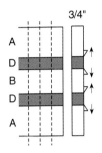

Figure 1
Sew all 5"-long strips together to make A-D-B-D-A strip set. Cut into 3/4"-wide segments as shown.

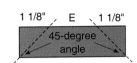

Figure 2
Measure in 1 1/8"; cut at a 45-degree angle.

Figure 3
Sew 2 C triangles to E to make roof section as shown.

Step 5. Sew a chimney section to a roof section, matching seams as shown in Figure 4; repeat for four sections. Press seams down and trim to 1/8".

Step 6. Sew an F strip to each side of G to make F-G-F unit. Cut into six 1 7/8"-wide pieced house front sections as shown in Figure 5.

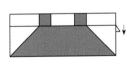

Figure 4
Join chimney and roof sections as shown.

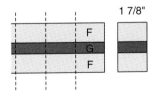

Figure 5
Cut F-G-F unit into 1 7/8" segments

Step 7. Sew house front section to chimney/roof section to complete one House block as shown in Figure 6; repeat to complete four blocks. Press seams down and trim to 1/8".

Step 8. Press blocks

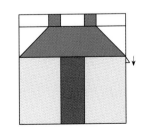

Figure 6
Sew a house section to a chimney/roof section to complete 1 House block as shown.

on both sides; square up to 2 3/4" x 2 3/4" if necessary.

Piecing Tree Blocks

Step 1. Prepare a template for pieces H-I and J using patterns given.

Step 2. Sew H and I strips together to make an H-I strip set. Cut two H-I units from strip; turn template and cut two I-H units as shown in Figure 7 for tree tops.

Step 3. Cut four J pieces from J strip, reversing template for four JR pieces as shown in Figure 8.

Step 4. Sew a J and JR to all the H-I and I-H units as shown in Figure 9.

Step 5. Sew 6"-long strips together to make K-L-K strip set. Press seams open; trim to 1/8". Cut four 1"-wide segments to make tree-trunk sections as shown in Figure 10.

Step 6. Center and sew one tree-trunk section to the bottom of each tree-top section as shown in Figure 11.

Step 7. Cut M strip into four 2 3/4"-wide segments.

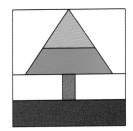

Tree 1
2 1/4" x 2 1/4" Block
Make 2

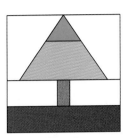

Tree 2
2 1/4" x 2 1/4" Block
Make 2

House
2 1/4" x 2 1/4" Block
Make 4

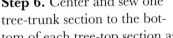

Figure 7
Cut 2 H-I and 2 I-H units from strip as shown.

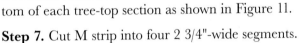

Figure 8
Cut J and JR pieces as shown.

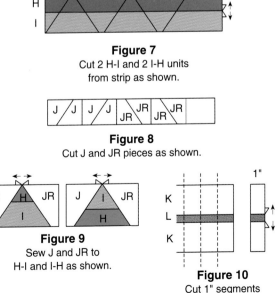

Figure 9
Sew J and JR to H-I and I-H as shown.

Figure 10
Cut 1" segments from K-L-K strip.

Sew an M segment to the bottom of each pieced unit to complete Tree blocks.

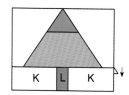

Figure 11
Sew a K-L-K segment to the bottom of tree-top sections.

Step 8. Press blocks on both sides; square up to 2 3/4" x 2 3/4" if necessary.

Piecing Center Block

Note: Press seams toward triangles and strips; trim all seams to 1/8".

Step 1. Cut O squares in half on one diagonal to make four O triangles.

Step 2. Sew an O triangle to each corner of an N square as shown in Figure 12; trim corners of N square to 1/8" seam allowance.

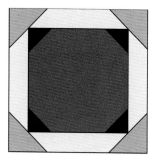

Center
2 1/4" x 2 1/4" Block
Make 1

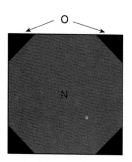

Figure 12
Sew O triangles to N.

Step 3. Sew a P strip to opposite sides of an O-N unit; sew P1 strips to the remaining sides as shown in Figure 13.

Step 4. Cut Q squares in half on one diagonal to make triangles. Sew Q to each side of the O-N-P

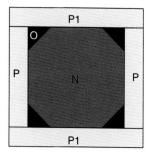

Figure 13
Sew P and P1 strips to the O-N unit.

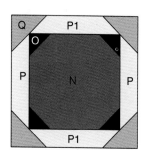

Figure 14
Sew Q to each side of the O-N-P unit.

unit as shown in Figure 14; trim seam allowance to 1/8" to complete the center block.

Step 5. Press block on both sides; square up to 2 3/4" x 2 3/4" if necessary.

Assembly

Step 1. Sew a House block to opposite sides of a Tree 1 block referring to the Placement Diagram for positioning of blocks to make a row; repeat for two rows.

Step 2. Sew a Tree 2 block to opposite sides of the center block referring to the Placement Diagram for positioning of blocks to make one row.

Step 3. Join the rows to complete pieced center.

Step 4. Sew R strips to opposite sides of the pieced center. Sew S strips to the remaining sides.

Step 5. Sew a T strip to opposite sides of the pieced center. Sew a U square to each short end of the remaining two T strips. Sew these strips to the remaining sides to complete pieced top.

Step 6. Press completed top on both sides; check for proper seam pressing and trim loose threads.

Finishing

Step 1. Prepare quilt top for quilting referring to General Instructions.

Step 2. Quilt as desired using white quilting thread.

Step 3. When quilting is complete, finish quilt referring to General Instructions using previously cut medium brown print binding strips to make straight-grain binding. ●

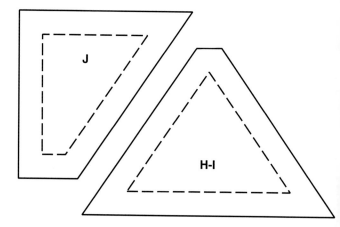

Snowball Tree Candle Mat

By Holly Daniels

his candle mat is a perfect accompaniment to your scented holiday candle as a centerpiece for your table. A basket of potpourri or a bowl of fruit would work as well.

- **Skill Level:** Beginner
- **Project Size:** 18" x 18"
- **Block Size:** 6" x 6"
- **Number of Blocks:** 9

- 1/4 yard each red and green prints
- 1/3 yard metallic print
- Backing 22" x 22"
- Thin batting 22" x 22"
- 2 1/4 yards self-made or purchased binding
- All-purpose thread to match fabrics
- 1 spool green rayon thread
- 1/8 yard fusible transfer web
- 4 wooden star buttons
- 28 assorted small buttons
- Basic sewing supplies and tools

Project Notes

Use wide-based candles or candles enclosed in glass on a fabric mat such as this one to prevent tipping. Place a protective plate underneath the candles to protect the mat from wax spills.

Instructions

Step 1. To make Nine-Patch blocks, cut two strips red print 2 1/2" by fabric width. Cut one strip into two 2 1/2" x 22" segments. Cut a 2 1/2" x 12" segment from the remaining strip; place remainder in your scrap bag.

Step 2. Cut two strips metallic print 2 1/2" by fabric width. Cut two 2 1/2" x 12" segments from one strip and one 2 1/2" x 22" segment from the second strip; place remainder in your scrap bag.

Step 3. Join fabric strips as shown in Figures 1 and 2 matching strip sizes; press all seams toward red print.

Step 4. Cut 22" strip set into eight 2 1/2" segments. Cut 12" strip set into four 2 1/2" segments.

Step 5. Join segments as shown in Figure 3 to make a Nine-Patch block; repeat for four blocks.

Step 6. To make Snowball blocks, cut one strip metallic print 6 1/2" x 33"; cut strip into 6 1/2" segments to make five squares. Cut a 9" x 10" segment

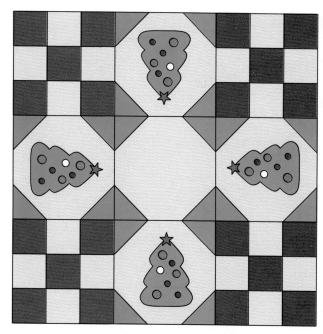

Snowball Tree Candle Mat
Placement Diagram
18" x 18"

Nine-Patch
6" x 6" Block

Snowball
6" x 6" Block

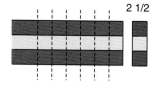

Figure 1
Join strips as shown.

Figure 2
Join strips as shown.

Figure 3
Join segments to make
a Nine-Patch block.

from one end of green print; set aside. Cut two 2 1/2" x 32" strips from remaining green print; cut strips into 2 1/2" segments to make 20 squares.

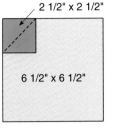
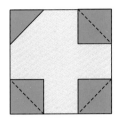

Figure 4
Sew on the diagonal of
the green square.

Figure 5
Stitch squares to each
corner as shown.

Step 7. Place one green print square on one corner of metallic print square, right sides together. Sew across the diagonal of the green print square as shown in Figure 4; trim away excess fabric from corner. Press seam toward corner; repeat on all corners to complete one block as shown in Figure 5. Repeat for five blocks.

Step 8. Following manufacturer's instructions, bond fusible transfer web to the wrong side of the 9" x 10" rectangle green print.

Step 9. Prepare template for tree using pattern piece given. Trace four trees onto paper side of fused fabric; cut out on traced lines. Remove paper backing.

Step 10. Center and fuse trees on each Snowball block.

Step 11. Using a machine zigzag stitch with green rayon thread in the top of the machine and matching all-purpose thread in the bobbin, stitch around each tree shape.

Step 12. Join two Nine-Patch blocks with one Snowball block with trees to make a row; press seams in one direction. Repeat for two rows. Join two Snowball blocks with trees with one Snowball block to make a row; press seams in one direction.

Step 13. Join block rows referring to the Placement Diagram to complete pieced top; press.

Step 14. Prepare top for quilting and finishing referring to General Instructions. **Note:** *Designer machine-quilted in a grid pattern using clear nylon monofilament in the top of the machine and all-purpose thread to match fabrics in the bobbin.*

Step 15. Hand-stitch a wooden star button to the top of each tree. Sew seven assorted buttons on each tree as embellishments. **Note:** *Trees may be embellished with embroidery stitches, sequins, ribbons, etc.* ●

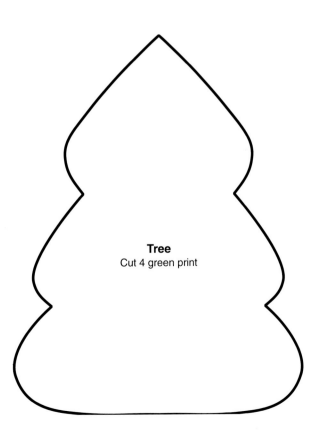

Tree
Cut 4 green print

Holly & Bows Tree Skirt

By Marian Shenk

I f you have a tiny Christmas tree, this small tree skirt will dress it up.

- **Skill Level:** Intermediate
- **Project Size:** Approximately 26" in diameter

- Scraps gold, red, blue and green prints
- 1 yard off-white print
- Backing 30" x 30"
- Batting 30" x 30"
- Coordinating all-purpose thread
- 1 1/2 yards 1/8"-wide gold braid
- Green 6-strand embroidery floss
- 40 (8mm) red beads
- 2 yards 1/4"-wide red velvet ribbon
- Hot glue gun
- Basic sewing supplies and tools

Holly & Bows Tree Skirt
Placement Diagram
Approximately 26" in
Diameter

Instructions

Step 1. Cut a 27"-diameter circle from backing, batting and off-white print.

Step 2. Fold off-white print circle in eighths as shown in Figure 1.

Step 3. Place template A center even with bottom

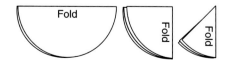

Figure 1
Fold circle in eighths.

edge; trace shape of A onto folded fabric. Cut on traced lines to make scalloped edge.

Step 4. Prepare templates for leaf and ornament shapes using pattern pieces given. Add a 1/8"–1/4" seam allowance all around when cutting each piece to turn under for hand appliqué. **Note:** *For machine-appliqué, cut pieces as given.*

Step 5. Cut 16 pieces gold braid 3 1/4" long. Hand-stitch two pieces to each ornament along lines marked on template using thread to match gold braid.

Step 6. Center, pin and baste one ornament shape and two leaf shapes in each of the eight segments referring to the Placement Diagram and photo of project for positioning suggestions.

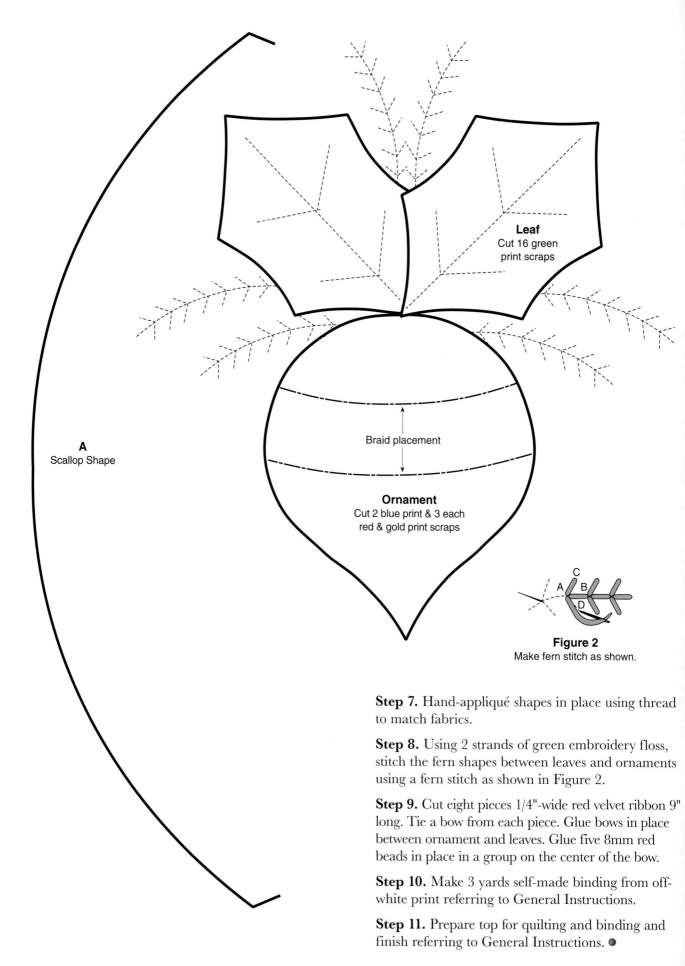

Leaf
Cut 16 green
print scraps

A
Scallop Shape

Braid placement

Ornament
Cut 2 blue print & 3 each
red & gold print scraps

Figure 2
Make fern stitch as shown.

Step 7. Hand-appliqué shapes in place using thread to match fabrics.

Step 8. Using 2 strands of green embroidery floss, stitch the fern shapes between leaves and ornaments using a fern stitch as shown in Figure 2.

Step 9. Cut eight pieces 1/4"-wide red velvet ribbon 9" long. Tie a bow from each piece. Glue bows in place between ornament and leaves. Glue five 8mm red beads in place in a group on the center of the bow.

Step 10. Make 3 yards self-made binding from off-white print referring to General Instructions.

Step 11. Prepare top for quilting and binding and finish referring to General Instructions. ●

Nativity Ornaments

By Holly Daniels

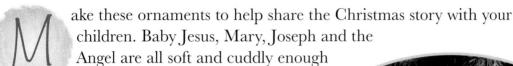

Make these ornaments to help share the Christmas story with your children. Baby Jesus, Mary, Joseph and the Angel are all soft and cuddly enough for even tiny children to hold.

- **Skill Level:** Beginner
- **Project Size:** Mary, Joseph and Angel 5" tall; Baby Jesus 3 1/2" tall

- 4 scraps muslin 4" x 6" for foundation
- 4 scraps 4" x 6" for backing
- 6" x 8" rectangle white-on-white print
- 5" x 5" square each blue and brown prints
- Scraps blue, white, beige, brown, gold and metallic prints and peach solid
- Polyester fiberfill
- 3" x 8" rectangle thin batting
- Coordinating all-purpose thread
- Black, brown and beige 6-strand embroidery floss
- Assorted white and gold buttons
- Basic sewing supplies and tools

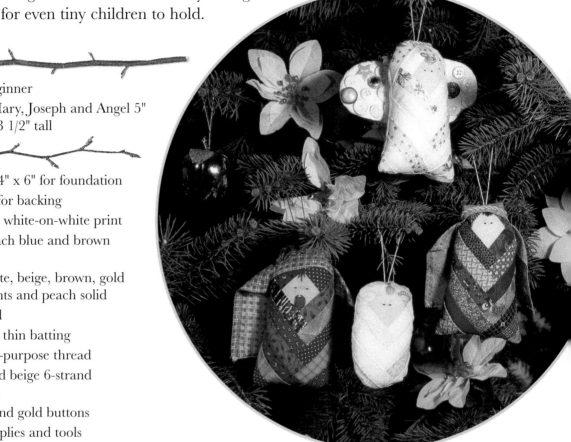

Project Note

If very small children will be playing with these ornaments, leave off the buttons on the angel's wings for safety purposes.

Instructions

Step 1. Trace ornament patterns; cut as directed on patterns. Transfer all lines onto scraps of muslin to make foundations. The marked side will be the front of the pattern.

Step 2. Cut each scrap of fabric at least 1/4" wider than each area to be covered. Use the following print scraps for each ornament: blue, Mary; white/beige, Baby Jesus; white/metallic, Angel; and brown/gold, Joseph.

Step 3. For each ornament, place a fabric scrap on the back of the pattern over area 1 using colors indicated in Step 2 and referring to pattern. Hold up to light to check placement. Place a piece of peach solid to fit area 2 over area 1 fabric with right sides together. Sew along the 1–2 line on the front of the pattern, beginning a few stitches before the line and extending into the seam allowance.

Step 4. Turn pattern over; trim seam allowance to 1/8". Flip peach solid to cover area 2; press.

Step 5. Continue adding fabric pieces in numerical

Joseph
Placement Diagram
5" tall

Mary
Placement Diagram
5" tall

Angel
Placement Diagram
5" tall

Baby Jesus
Placement Diagram
3 1/2" tall

order until entire ornament is covered. Trim along outer line.

Step 6. Using 3 strands of black or brown embroidery floss, make straight stitches for eyes on each ornament referring to the Placement Diagram and patterns for positioning.

Step 7. For Mary, make six straight stitches for hair using 6 strands of brown embroidery floss. For Joseph, make three straight stitches for hair, 13 straight stitches for beard and two straight stitches for mustache using 6 strands of brown embroidery floss referring to Figure 1 for positioning.

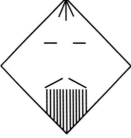

Figure 1
Stitch beard and mustache as shown.

Step 8. To make hair on Baby Jesus and Angel ornaments, use 6 strands beige embroidery floss to make three 1/2"-long loop stitches.

Step 9. To make hanging loop for Angel ornament, cut one 10" piece beige embroidery floss. Fold floss, matching ends, to make a loop. Pin the loop to the top of the front side of the Angel ornament. Place pieced ornament front and backing fabric right sides together; stitch around seams leaving a small opening where marked on pattern. Clip curves and turn right side out. Smooth seams; stuff. Hand-stitch opening closed. Repeat on Baby Jesus ornament to finish. Stitch Mary and Joseph ornaments without hanging loops.

Step 10. For angel's wings, fold the 6" x 8" piece white-on-white print right sides together to form a 3" x 8" rectangle. Place the 3" x 8" piece thin batting on the bottom. Trace wing shape onto fabric side. Sew along line; trim to 1/4" seam allowance.

Step 11. Cut a hole through one layer of fabric only as marked on wing pattern. Clip seams; turn right side ou through cut opening. Press lightly. Sew buttons to wing in random pattern in the areas marked on pattern.

Step 12. Stitch wings to back of Angel ornament.

Step 13. To make halo, cut three pieces beige

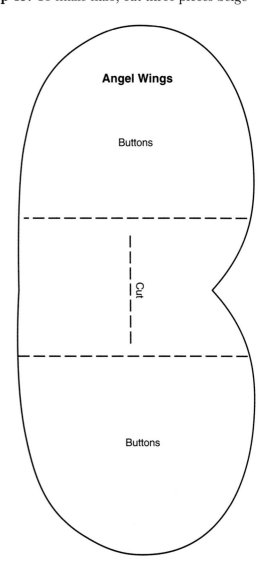

Angel Wings

Buttons

Cut

Buttons

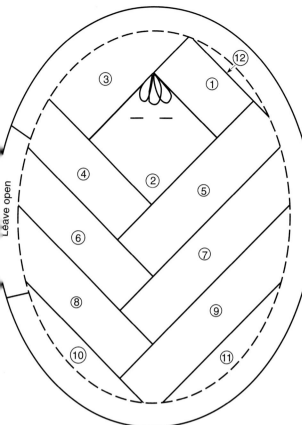

Baby Jesus Ornament Pattern
Cut 1 each backing & muslin

ment and then through headpiece and back to ornament, leaving 3–4" hanging loop; knot to hold. Fold headpiece back down.

Step 16. Make rope tie for headpiece referring to halo instructions in Step 13 except tie two knots 8" apart. Tack to top of head over headpiece with knot hanging in back to finish.

Step 17. For Joseph's headpiece, repeat Steps 14–16 using 5" x 5" square brown print for headpiece, a 10" piece brown embroidery floss for hanging loop and one 24" length each brown and beige embroidery floss for rope tie. ●

embroidery floss 24" long. Tie together on one end. Twist the strands together to make a tight twist. Fold twisted strand back onto itself, allowing two twisted strands to twist together. Tie two knots 6" apart; trim ends to 1/2". Tie rope around head; tie in back and tack to top of head.

Step 14. For Mary's headpiece, fold edges of all sides of the 5" x 5" square blue print under 1/4" and stitch for hem. Find center of one side of square; line up with center of ornament front. Insert straight pin in forehead area to hold. Fold top ends to back as shown in Figure 2; tack ends in place behind head. Bring fabric forward over ear area; tack in place.

Step 15. Cut a 10" piece beige embroidery floss. Flip headpiece up; stitch through orna-

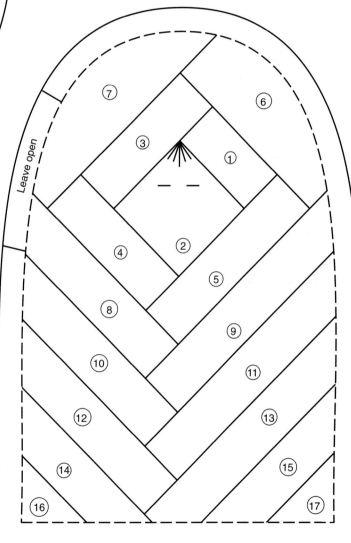

Mary, Joseph & Angel Ornaments Pattern
Cut 1 each backing & muslin

Figure 2
Fold Mary's headpiece as shown.

Dove & Hearts Christmas Stocking

By Jodi G. Warner

T he dove carries an olive branch to share his message of peace with the world. The hearts convey a message of love, and the checkerboard patches add a touch of country.

Dove & Hearts Christmas Stocking
Placement Diagram

- **Skill Level:** Intermediate
- **Stocking Size:** 8 1/2" x 16 1/2"

- Scraps of the following fabrics: 2 red plaid (hearts), 2 contrasting cream-on-cream prints (dove, checkerboard), 1 black print (checkerboard) and 1 forest green print (center patchwork)
- 1 fat eighth beige print for background
- 1/3 yard medium green print for cuff, center patchwork and backing
- 3/8 yard red print for narrow borders, small squares and binding
- 1 square 7" x 7" red solid for piping
- 2 pieces 10" x 18" for linings
- 2 pieces thin batting 10" x 18"
- All-purpose thread to match fabrics
- Contrasting quilting thread
- Scrap lightweight fusible transfer web
- Scrap fabric stabilizer
- Green machine-embroidery thread
- 1 1/4 yards 1/8"-wide cording
- 1/4" black button
- Manila-folder-weight paper
- Basic sewing supplies and tools and water-soluble fabric marker

Instructions

Step 1. Cut beige print as follows: two squares 2 3/4" x 2 3/4" for D, one square 4 1/2" x 4 1/2" for E, one strip 1" x 7 1/2" for F and one strip 2 1/4" x 7 3/4" for G. Cut E squares in half on one diagonal to make two E triangles.

Step 2. Cut two squares medium green print 3 1/2" x 3 1/2" for A, eight strips forest green print 1 1/2" x 3 1/2" for B and six squares red print 1 1/2" x 1 1/2" for C.

Step 3. Sew B to opposite sides of A; sew C to each end of one B strip and sew to A-B as shown in Figure 1. Sew C to one end of one B strip; sew to the previously pieced unit as shown in Figure 2. Repeat to make a second A-B-C unit.

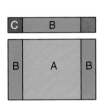

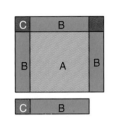

Figure 1
Sew C-B unit to
B-A unit as shown.

Figure 2
Sew C-B to previously
pieced unit.

Step 4. Place pieced A-B-C units right sides together as shown in Figure 3. Make a template for piece X. Lay X on layered A-B-C units; draw a line along long edge of X. Remove template; stitch on marked line as shown in Figure 4; trim 1/4" away from stitching line. Press stitched section.

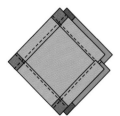

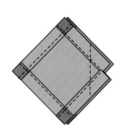

Figure 3
Place pieced units
right sides together.

Figure 4
Stitch along drawn line.

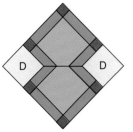

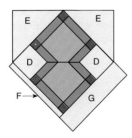

Figure 5
Set in D as shown.

Figure 6
Add E, F and G as shown.

Step 5. Set D into pieced section as shown in Figure 5. Sew E to two adjacent corners and F and G to opposite adjacent corners to finish center panel as shown in Figure 6; press and set aside.

Step 6. For cuff checkerboard panel, cut one strip each of one cream-on-cream print and black print 1 1/4" x 13". Join strips along length; press seams toward black strip. Cut into ten 1 1/4" segments. Join segments as shown in Figure 7 to make a checkerboard panel.

Figure 7
Join segments as shown to make a
checkerboard panel.

Step 7. For toe checkerboard panel, cut two strips each of one cream-on-cream print and black print 1 1/4" x 11 1/2". Join strips in alternating order along length; press seams toward black strips. Cut into nine 1 1/4" segments. Join segments as shown in Figure 8 to make toe panel.

Figure 8
Join segments as shown to make toe panel.

Step 8. Cut three strips red print 7/8" x 8 1/4" for H and one strip medium green print 2 3/8" x 8 1/4" for I.

Step 9. Sew an H strip to the top and bottom of the pieced center panel; press seams toward H. Sew the toe checkerboard panel to the bottom and the cuff checkerboard panel to the top of the pieced section as shown in Figure 9; add H and I to the top. Press pieced section.

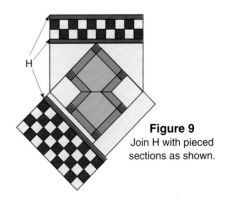

Figure 9
Join H with pieced
sections as shown.

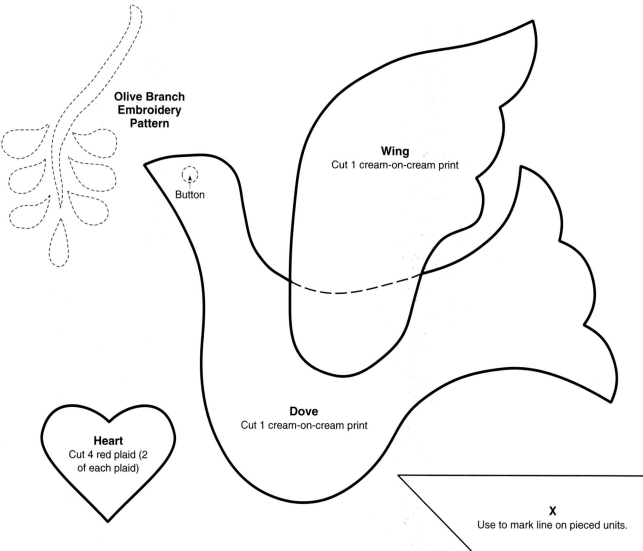

Olive Branch Embroidery Pattern

Wing
Cut 1 cream-on-cream print

Button

Dove
Cut 1 cream-on-cream print

Heart
Cut 4 red plaid (2 of each plaid)

X
Use to mark line on pieced units.

Step 10. Make a template for the dove, wing and heart using full-size patterns given. Trace four hearts, one wing and one dove onto paper side of a scrap of lightweight fusible transfer web. Cut out shapes leaving a margin around each piece. Fuse to wrong sides of fabric scraps as indicated on patterns for fabric colors. Cut out shapes on traced lines; remove paper backing.

Step 11. Fuse one heart to the wing referring to the Placement Diagram for positioning. Fuse three hearts on I and the dove and wing with heart on pieced panel again referring to the Placement Diagram for positioning.

Step 12. Cut pieces of fabric stabilizer slightly larger than the appliqué areas. Pin or baste against the wrong side of work directly under appliqué areas.

Step 13. Using all-purpose thread to match fabrics and a medium-width zigzag stitch, machine-appliqué around appliqué shapes. When appliqué is complete, remove basting or pins and fabric stabilizer along stitching lines around and within all appliqués.

Step 14. Layer one lining piece with batting and pieced stocking front. Hand-quilt next to patchwork seams and appliqué edges and as desired using contrasting quilting thread.

Step 15. Cut a backing piece 10" x 18" from medium green print. Mark a 1" on-point grid onto the piece. Layer backing piece with remaining batting and lining pieces; pin or baste. Machine-quilt on marked lines with all-purpose thread.

Step 16. Sew the 1/4" black button on the dove as marked on pattern for eye. Transfer pattern for olive branch embroidery to stocking using pattern given and a water-soluble marker. Using green machine-embroidery thread, satin-stitch stem and leaves.

Step 17. Finish stocking referring to Steps 18–22 for Homespun Patches Stocking on page 30 and using stocking pattern given on page 31. ●

Homespun Patches Christmas Stocking

By Jodi G. Warner

Four-Patches and hearts combine with strip piecing to make this small stocking with a homespun look. Add buttons and snaps for trim and your stocking is complete.

- **Skill Level:** Intermediate
- **Stocking Size:** 8 1/2" x 16 1/2"

- Scraps of the following prints: 4 reds (hearts), beige (background), cream-on-cream (patchwork) and forest green (patchwork)
- 1/3 yard medium green print for Four-Patch background and backing
- 3/8 yard red print for cuff, toe strips, checkerboard and binding
- 1 square 7" x 7" red solid for piping
- 2 pieces 10" x 18" for lining
- 2 pieces thin batting 10" x 18"
- All-purpose thread to match fabrics
- Contrasting quilting thread
- Scrap lightweight fusible transfer web
- Scrap fabric stabilizer
- Red and green 6-strand embroidery floss
- 1 1/4 yards 1/8"-wide cording
- 2 (3/4") red heart buttons
- Large black snap size 4/0
- Manila-folder-weight paper
- Basic sewing supplies and tools

Instructions

Step 1. For one patchwork heart, use a different red print scrap to cut each of the following pieces: C—1 1/4" x 1 1/4" square; D—1 1/2" x 2 1/4" rectangle; E—1 1/4" x 2 1/4" rectangle; and F—1 1/4" x 3" rectangle. Repeat cutting for a second patchwork heart.

Step 2. Sew C to D matching one end as shown in Figure 1; trim away D seam allowance above C as shown in Figure 1. Sew C-D to E and add F to complete one patchwork heart as shown in Figure 2; repeat for second patchwork heart.

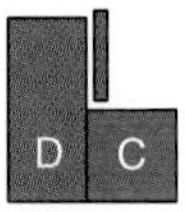

Figure 1
Trim away D seam
allowance above C.

Figure 2
Sew C-D to E and add F to
complete 1 patchwork heart.

Step 3. For one Four-Patch block, cut two squares each cream-on-cream and forest green prints 1 1/2" x 1 1/2" for G; repeat cutting for a second block. Join squares as shown in Figure 3 to make a Four-Patch block; repeat for a second Four-Patch block.

Figure 3
Join squares as shown to
make a Four-Patch block.

4 1/4" x 4 3/4"	4 1/4" x 4 3/4"
4 3/4" x 5 1/2"	4 1/4" x 4 3/4"

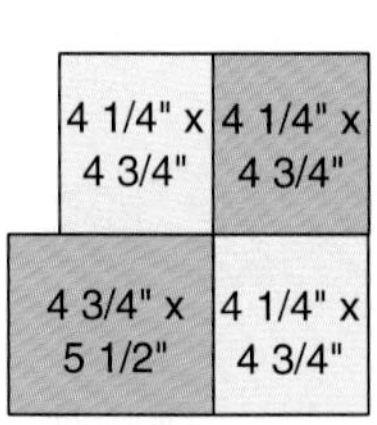

Figure 4
Join rectangles to make
center background section.

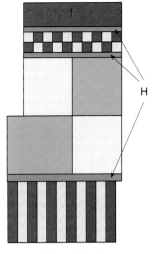

for II. Cut a red print rectangle 2 1/4" x 8 1/4" for I.

Step 9. Sew an H strip to the top and bottom of the pieced center panel; press seams toward H. Sew the toe striped panel to the bottom and the cuff checkerboard panel to the top of the pieced section; add H and I to the top as shown in Figure 6. Press pieced section.

Figure 6
Join sections as shown.

Step 10. Make a template for the patchwork heart using full-size pattern given. Trace onto paper side of a scrap of lightweight fusible transfer web. Draw two 2 1/2" x 2 1/2" squares onto paper side of a scrap of fusible transfer web. Cut out shapes on traced lines; fuse to wrong side of fabric patchwork hearts and Four-Patch blocks. Remove paper backing.

Step 11. Place patchwork hearts and Four-Patch blocks on medium green print and beige print rectangles referring to the Placement Diagram for positioning. Fuse in place.

Step 12. Cut pieces of fabric stabilizer slightly larger than the appliqué areas. Pin or baste against the wrong side of work directly under appliqué areas.

Step 13. Using all-purpose thread to match fabrics and a medium-width zigzag stitch, machine-appliqué around patchwork shapes. When appliqué is complete, remove basting or pins and fabric stabilizer along stitching lines around and within all appliqués.

Step 14. Layer one lining piece with batting and pieced stocking front. Hand-quilt next to patchwork seams and appliqué edges using contrasting quilting thread.

Step 15. Cut a backing piece 10" x 18" from medium green print. Mark a 1" on-point grid onto the piece. Layer backing piece with remaining batting and lining pieces; pin or baste. Machine-quilt on marked lines with all-purpose thread.

Step 16. Sew a 3/4" red heart button in the center of each Four-Patch block and separated snap pieces at patchwork heart centers using 6 strands of red embroidery floss for snaps and 6 strands of green embroidery floss for buttons.

Step 17. Stitch 6-strand red embroidery floss X's on

Step 4. Cut one rectangle medium green print and two rectangles beige print 4 1/4" x 4 3/4" and one rectangle medium green print 4 3/4" x 5 1/2". Join rectangles as shown in Figure 4 to make center background section; press.

Step 5. For cuff checkerboard panel, cut one strip each cream-on-cream and red prints 1 1/4" x 13". Join strips along one long edge; press seams toward red strip. Cut into ten 1 1/4" segments.

Step 6. Join segments as shown in Figure 5 to make a checkerboard panel.

Figure 5
Join segments as shown to make a checkerboard panel.

Step 7. For toe panel, cut six strips red print and five strips cream-on-cream print 1 1/4" x 4 1/2". Join strips along length, alternating colors; press seams toward red print.

Step 8. Cut three strips forest green print 7/8" x 9"

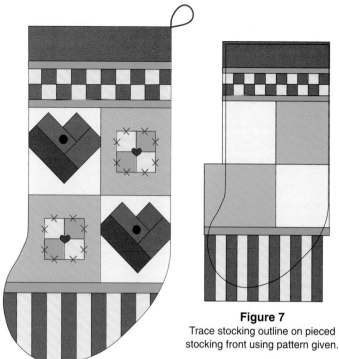

Homespun Patches Christmas Stocking
Placement Diagram
8 1/2" x 16 1/2"

Figure 7
Trace stocking outline on pieced
stocking front using pattern given.

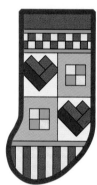

Figure 8
Position piping on stocking
front cutting line.

Stocking Pattern

Add 8" between pieces when cutting to make complete pattern.

edges of Four-Patch blocks referring to
Placement Diagram for positioning.

Step 18. Trace stocking outline on
pieced stocking front using pattern
given referring to Figure 7.

Step 19. Cut 1"-wide bias strips
from red solid; sew together on short
ends to make one strip 45" long.
Fold strip with wrong sides together,
inserting cording along fold; machine-baste through
fabric layers close to cording using a zipper foot.
Trim excess seam allowance past stitching to 1/4".
With piping pointing inward, position and baste on
stocking front as shown in Figure 8, stitching exactly
over stocking front seam line. Taper piping ends into
seam allowance at top opening seam lines.

Step 20. Lay stocking front over quilted back with
lining sides out. Stitch around following basted piping outline; lock stitches at opening edges. Trim
away excess to 1/4"; trim top edges even and overcast
raw seam edges. Turn right side out.

Step 21. Prepare a 20" length of 3/8" double-fold bias
binding from red print as follows: Cut a 1 1/2" x 20" bias
strip from red print. Lay a 3/4"-wide strip of manila-folder-weight paper down the center wrong side of bias strip;
press both raw edges over paper. Slide paper along strip
to complete single-fold press of entire length. Align

creased edges right side out; press for double-fold bias
tape. ***Note:*** *A 3/4" bias-tape maker may be used. Cut a
4 1/2" piece for loop; stitched folded edges together.*

Step 22. Place loop ends together; machine-baste
over seam at upper right side of stocking opening,
loop facing down. Apply binding to top opening
edge, beginning at center back. Fold one end under;
overlap other end when they meet to finish. ●

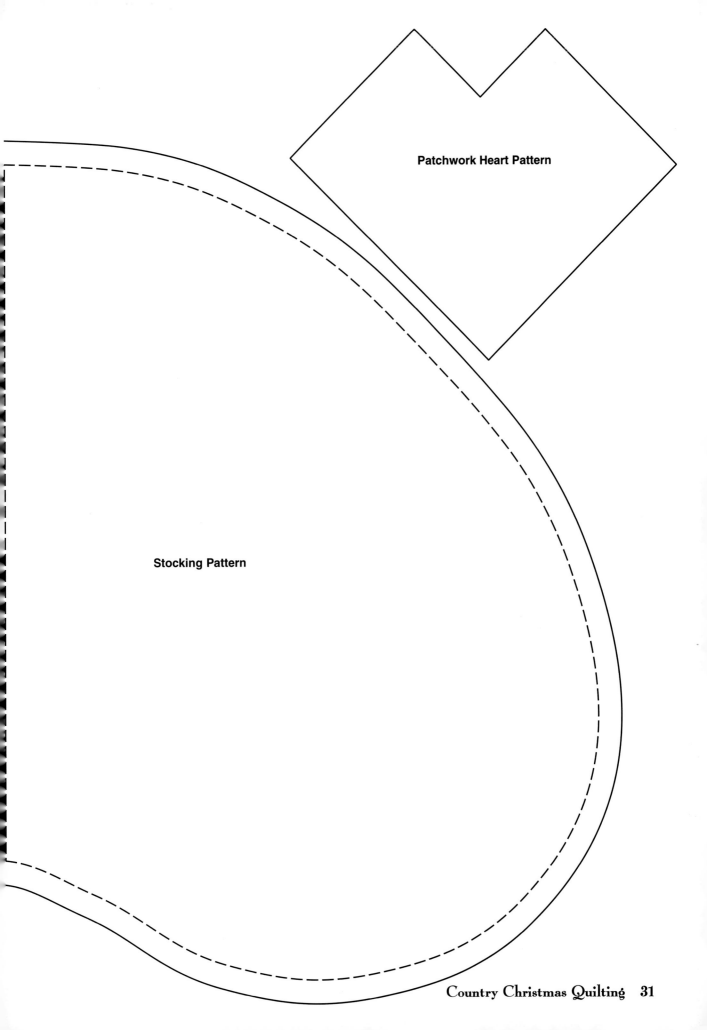

Patchwork Heart Pattern

Stocking Pattern

3-D Diamond Ornaments

By Norma Storm

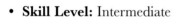

Mostly Log Cabin style, these soft, colorful patchwork ornaments may be carefully planned or made with scraps in a random fashion. Add embellishments to give each ornament a unique look.

- **Skill Level:** Intermediate
- **Project Size:** Ornament A—3 1/4" x 5 1/2", Ornaments B and C—3 7/8" x 6 1/2"

- Scraps red, green, white and yellow fabrics
- Small amount of polyester fiberfill
- 14" x 14" piece lightweight batting
- Coordinating all-purpose thread
- 1/2 yard cording for hangers
- Embellishments such as bells, beads and ribbon
- Tracing paper
- Basic sewing supplies and tools

Project Notes

By turning the designs upside down or using different colors and trim, these ornaments may be made as plain or as fancy as you wish. When stuffed they are puffy, but they are just as attractive when unstuffed as shown by one example in the photo.

You may choose from a variety of different materials for the ornaments' hangers. Pearl cotton, 6-strand embroidery floss, metallic cording and ribbon would all work well. Purchase the amount indicated in the Materials as cording.

Embroidery or quilting stitches may be added to give even more detail to these already pretty ornaments.

Instructions

Step 1. Trace paper-piecing patterns given onto tracing

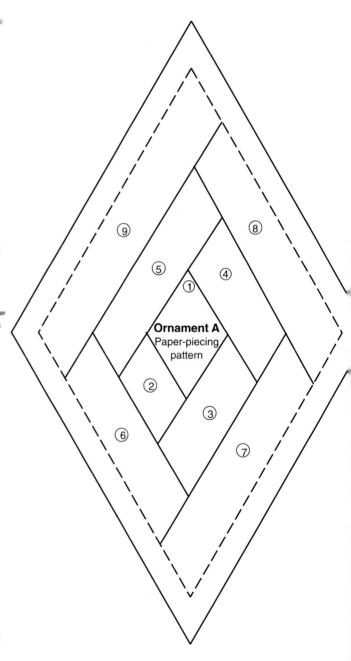

Ornament A
Paper-piecing
pattern

paper, transferring all lines and numbers. Make four copies of chosen pattern for each ornament. Prepare template for Ornament C; cut as directed on pattern.

Step 2. Cut 1 1/2"-wide strips of fabric from fabric scraps for every piece on Ornament A and 2"-wide strips for Ornament B. Cut strips in random widths for Ornament C.

Step 3. For ornaments A and B, place a fabric strip in the piece 1 position on the unlined side of the tracing paper; pin in place. Check to see that the piece completely covers the space with at least 1/8" extra all around line. Place piece 2 on top of piece 1 with right sides together referring to Figure 1. Sew

along traced line through fabric and paper.

Step 4. Press piece 2 flat referring to Figure 2; add piece 3 in the same manner. Continue adding pieces in numerical order and pressing flat until paper pattern is covered. Trim edges of fabric even with edge of pattern. Repeat for four sections for each ornament.

Step 5. For Ornament C, stitch strips diagonally across the batting pieces to completely cover batting. Repeat for four sections. Machine-quilt in the ditch of seams.

Step 6. Sew two pieced units together along one side. Add a third pieced unit to one side; add fourth pieced unit to one side. Join the remaining sides, leaving a 2"–3" opening on one side to turn right side out. Trim points and threads. Turn right side out.

Step 7. Cut a 6" piece of cording for each ornament. Fold and sew together ends to one pointed end of ornament for hanging.

Step 8. Stuff ornament with polyester fiberfill through opening. Hand-stitch opening closed to finish. **Note:** *Omit stuffing to make a flat, three-dimensional ornament.*

Step 9. Embellishments such as beads, bells or ribbon bows may be stitched to ornaments to give each one a unique look. ●

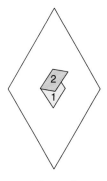

Figure 1
Place piece 2 right sides
together with piece 1.

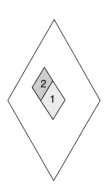

Figure 2
Press piece 2 flat.

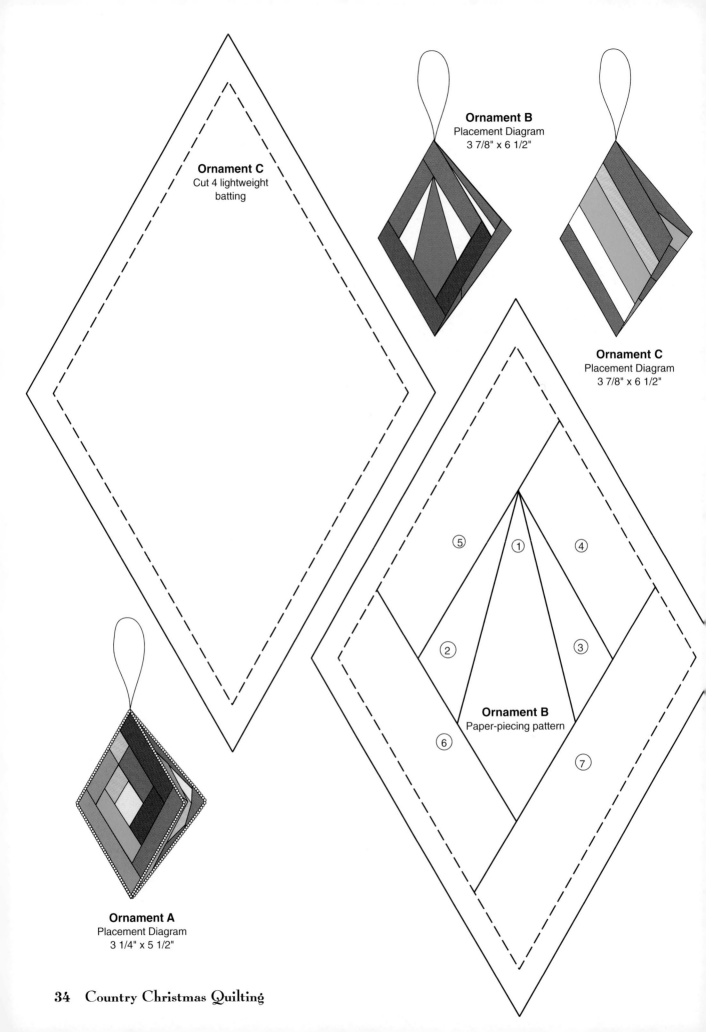

Ornament C
Cut 4 lightweight
batting

Ornament B
Placement Diagram
3 7/8" x 6 1/2"

Ornament C
Placement Diagram
3 7/8" x 6 1/2"

⑤ ① ④

② ③

Ornament B
Paper-piecing pattern

⑥ ⑦

Ornament A
Placement Diagram
3 1/4" x 5 1/2"

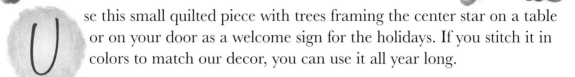

Star So Bright

By Carla Schwab

Use this small quilted piece with trees framing the center star on a table or on your door as a welcome sign for the holidays. If you stitch it in colors to match our decor, you can use it all year long.

- **Skill Level:** Beginner
- **Project Size:** 17" x 17"
- **Block Size:** 6 1/4" x 6 1/4"
- **Number of Blocks:** 4

- 1/8 yard each medium yellow, brown, blue and light green prints
- 1/4 yard each dark green, red and yellow prints
- Backing 21" x 21"
- Batting 21" x 21"
- 2 1/4 yards self-made or purchased binding
- Coordinating all-purpose thread
- Basic sewing supplies and tools

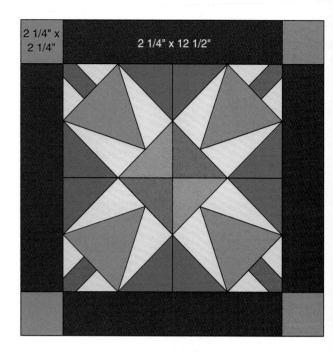

Star So Bright
Placement Diagram
17" x 17"

Instructions

Step 1. Prepare templates using pattern pieces given. Cut as directed on each piece for one block; repeat for four blocks.

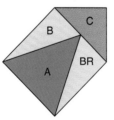

Star So Bright
6 1/4" x 6 1/4" Block

Step 2. To piece one block, sew B and BR to A; press seams toward A. Sew a medium yellow C to the A-B unit referring to Figure 1; press seam toward C. Sew a blue C to the B and BR sides of the A-B-C unit; press seams toward C pieces.

Figure 1
Sew a medium yellow C to the A-B unit.

Step 3. To make tree trunk for appliqué, cut four brown print rectangles 2 1/2" x 3". Fold in half along length with right sides together; stitch along 3" side. Trim seam; turn right side out. Center seam on backside; press.

Step 4. Baste tree trunk piece to light green C triangle, centering tree trunk piece with seam side down, referring to Figure 2; trim trunk piece even with triangle.

Step 5. Sew the light green C tree trunk piece to the remaining edge of A to complete one block as shown in Figure 3; press seam toward C. Repeat for four blocks.

Step 6. Join four blocks with yellow print C triangles in the center to make pieced center referring to

Figure 2
Baste tree trunk piece to green C.

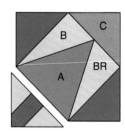

Figure 3
Sew tree trunk C piece to the A-B-C unit to complete 1 block.

the Placement Diagram for positioning. Press seams in one direction.

Step 7. Cut four strips red print 2 3/4" x 13" and four squares dark green print 2 3/4" x 2 3/4". Sew a square to each end of two strips; press seams toward squares.

Step 8. Sew a 2 3/4" x 13" red print strip to opposite sides of the pieced center; press seams toward strips. Sew the strips with squares to the remaining sides; press seams toward strips.

Step 9. Hand-appliqué tree trunk pieces in place on C pieces; remove basting.

Step 10. Mark quilting design given on borders of quilt and in the A pieces as marked on template.

Step 11. Prepare top for quilting and binding referring to General Instructions. ●

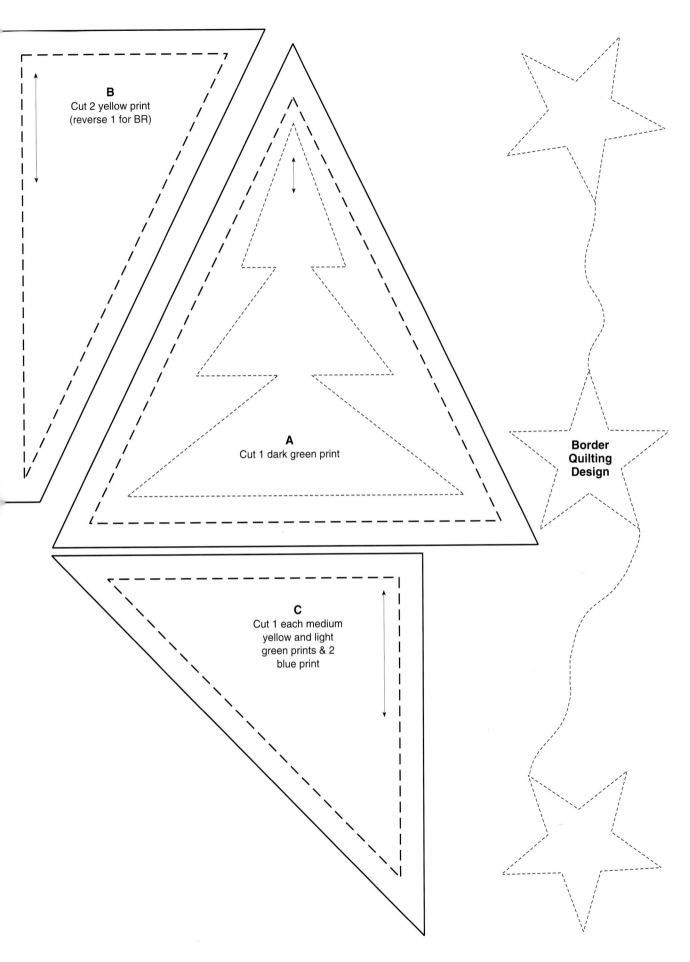

B
Cut 2 yellow print
(reverse 1 for BR)

A
Cut 1 dark green print

C
Cut 1 each medium
yellow and light
green prints & 2
blue print

**Border
Quilting
Design**

Poinsettia Lace Ornaments

By Marian Shenk

Small fabric scraps combine with a variety of embellishments to create these neat Christmas ornaments. You'll want to make several sets and share them with your family and friends.

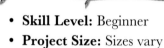

- **Skill Level:** Beginner
- **Project Size:** Sizes vary

Bird Ornament
Placement Diagram
Approximately 5" x 4"

Heart Ornament
Placement Diagram
Approximately 4" x 3 1/2"

Bell Ornament
Placement Diagram
Approximately 4" x 3 3/4"

- Scraps of red fabrics
- Scraps of white felt
- Scrap white fur 3" x 6"
- 1/2 yard 1 1/4"-wide white beading lace
- 1/2 yard 1/4"-wide green satin ribbon
- 1 yard 1/8"-wide gold cording
- 6 sets small silk holly leaves grouped in threes
- 6 (1") silk poinsettias
- Small amount of polyester fiberfill
- Coordinating all-purpose thread
- 4 (3/8") red metallic pompoms
- 1/2 yard 2 1/2"-wide white lace
- 1/4 yard 1 1/2"-wide red plaid ribbon
- 1/4" gold bell
- 1/2 yard black 6-strand embroidery floss
- Yellow marker
- Hot glue gun
- Basic sewing supplies and tools, yellow marker and black permanent fabric pen

Stocking Ornament
Placement Diagram
Approximately 3 1/2" x 4 1/2"

Snowman Ornament
Placement Diagram
Approximately 2 1/2" x 6"

Instructions

Step 1. Prepare templates for each ornament using pattern pieces given. Cut as directed on each piece.

Step 2. Using lace placement lines on templates for bell, stocking and heart, cut a piece of white 1 1/4"-wide beading lace 6" long for each ornament. Cut a piece of 1/4"-wide green satin ribbon the same length. Thread ribbon through beading lace.

Step 3. Transfer lace placement lines to fabric. Center beading lace with ribbon on lines; pin in place. Stitch in place on both sides of center area of beading lace; trim ends to size of ornament.

Step 4. Cut five pieces 1/8"-wide gold cording 5" long.

Fold cording in half; pin to top of each ornament referring to Figure 1 and X on patterns for placement.

Step 5. Place pairs of ornament pieces right sides together. Sew all around, leaving a 1" opening as indicated on patterns. Trim seams; clip curves. Turn right side out.

Figure 1
Place folded cording on ornament as shown.

Figure 2
Stitch snowman hat piece as shown.

Step 6. Stuff each ornament lightly, filling all points, using polyester fiberfill. Hand-stitch all openings closed except for the bird ornament.

Step 7. For bird ornament, cut three pieces 2 1/2"-wide white lace 6" long; gather ends of two pieces tightly for wings. Hand-stitch wings on both sides of bird referring to lines on pattern for placement. Insert the third piece in the opening left at the tail before hand-stitching closed. Sew a French knot using 3 strands of black embroidery floss to make eyes, pulling stitches from one side to the other to make an indent for each eye. Make beak using yellow marker.

Step 8. Sew snowman's hat together along seam line as shown in Figure 2; turn right side out. Glue on top of snowman's head. Glue 1/2" x 3 1/2" strip white fur to bottom edge of hat to cover raw edges.

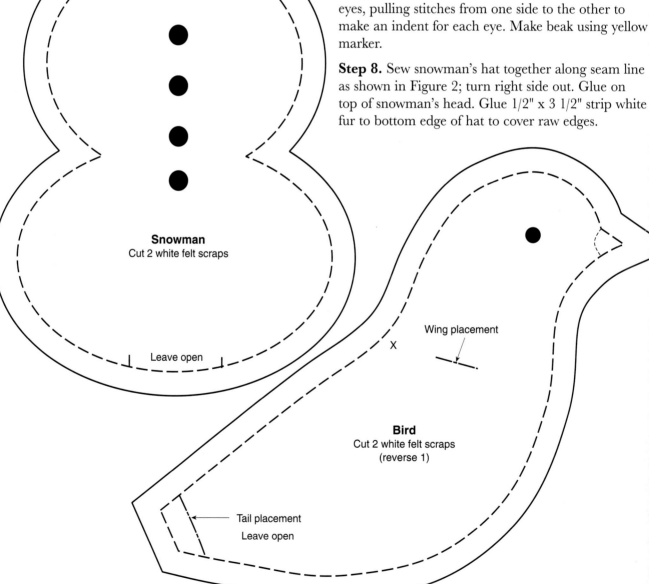

Snowman
Cut 2 white felt scraps

Leave open

Wing placement

X

Bird
Cut 2 white felt scraps
(reverse 1)

Tail placement
Leave open

Fold cording in half; pin to top of each ornament referring to Figure 1 and X on patterns for placement.

Step 5. Place pairs of ornament pieces right sides together. Sew all around, leaving a 1" opening as indicated on patterns. Trim seams; clip curves. Turn right side out.

Figure 1
Place folded cording on ornament as shown.

Figure 2
Stitch snowman hat piece as shown.

Step 6. Stuff each ornament lightly, filling all points, using polyester fiberfill. Hand-stitch all openings closed except for the bird ornament.

Step 7. For bird ornament, cut three pieces 2 1/2"-wide white lace 6" long; gather ends of two pieces tightly for wings. Hand-stitch wings on both sides of bird referring to lines on pattern for placement. Insert the third piece in the opening left at the tail before hand-stitching closed. Sew a French knot using 3 strands of black embroidery floss to make eyes, pulling stitches from one side to the other to make an indent for each eye. Make beak using yellow marker.

Step 8. Sew snowman's hat together along seam line as shown in Figure 2; turn right side out. Glue on top of snowman's head. Glue 1/2" x 3 1/2" strip white fur to bottom edge of hat to cover raw edges.

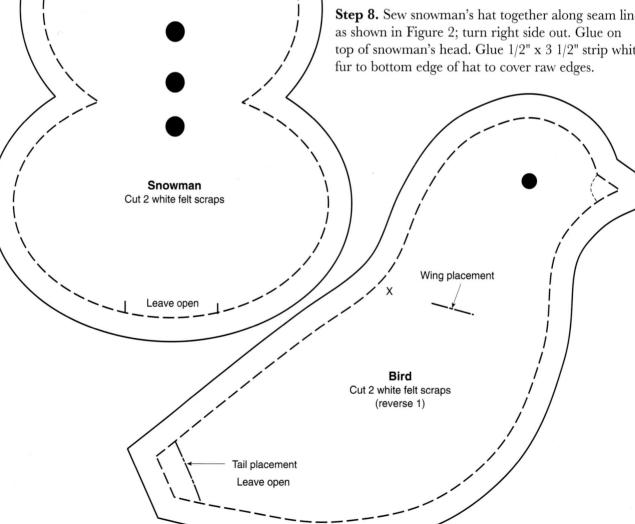

Snowman
Cut 2 white felt scraps

Leave open

Wing placement

X

Bird
Cut 2 white felt scraps
(reverse 1)

Tail placement
Leave open

Step 9. Whipstitch the ends of a 1" x 6" piece white fur together to make a tube for the top of the stocking. Glue fur piece in place around top edge of stocking.

Step 10. Glue the holly leaves and poinsettias to top of bell, stocking and heart, at the top of each wing on bird and on the snowman's hat, referring to the Placement Diagrams and photo of ornaments for positioning.

Step 11. Glue four 3/8" red metallic pompoms to the snowman's body referring to the pattern for placement. Fold the 1/4-yard piece of red plaid ribbon in half lengthwise. Stitch together along length to make a tube; turn right side out. Press with seam on side. Turn in ends; hand-stitch closed, pulling thread to gather ends a little. Tie the stitched ribbon around the snowman's neck to make a scarf.

Step 12. Mark face on snowman using black permanent fabric pen to finish. ●

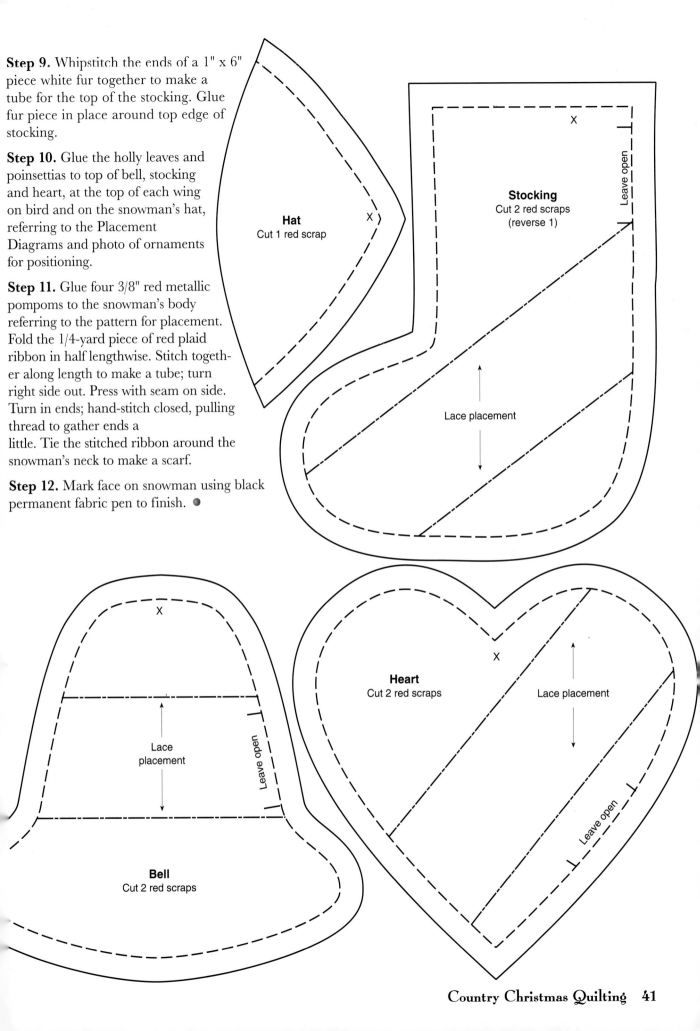

Hat
Cut 1 red scrap

X

Stocking
Cut 2 red scraps
(reverse 1)

X

Leave open

Lace placement

Bell
Cut 2 red scraps

X

Lace placement

Leave open

Heart
Cut 2 red scraps

X

Lace placement

Leave open

Buttons & Stars Garland

By Ann Boyce

Make this easy garland to hang on your tree or place on your mantel to complement your patchwork ornaments.

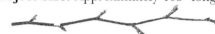

- **Skill Level:** Beginner
- **Project Size:** Approximately 105" long

Instructions

Step 1. Bond 18" x 18" square fusible transfer web to wrong side of the 18" x 18" square red check.

Step 2. Prepare template for star shape using pattern given. Trace 36 stars on the paper side of the fused fabric. Cut out on traced lines using pinking shears; remove paper backing.

Step 3. Fuse 18 red check stars to the square of cotton batting, leaving 1/2" between stars.

Step 4. Cut out fused fabric/batting stars 1/4" larger than the fabric star all around.

Step 5. Leaving a 3" tail or longer, if desired, place cording along the center of the batting side of a

- 1 square red check 18" x 18"
- Cotton batting 18" x 18"
- 1 spool white all-purpose thread
- 1/2 yard fusible transfer web
- 36 (1/2") white buttons
- 3 1/2 yards red 1/8" cording
- Basic sewing supplies and tools and pinking shears

Small Star
Cut 36 red check

Buttons & Stars Garland
Placement Diagram
Approximately 105" long

fused fabric/batting star. Place a fabric star on top of cording and fuse in place as shown in Figure 1. Continue fusing fabric stars to fabric/batting stars with cording between, leaving 3" of cording between stars, until all stars are used.

Step 6. Trim remaining end to same length as beginning tail and tie a knot in each end.

Step 7. Sew a white 1/2" button on both sides of each star, sewing both buttons on at the same time using white all-purpose thread to finish. ●

Figure 1
Center cording on the batting side of a fused fabric/batting star; place fabric star on top and fuse in place.

Crazy Patchwork Angel

By Tamela Meredith Partidge

Try this easy angel design in a variety of fabrics to celebrate any holiday or season. This scrappy angel looks good on your tree or nestled among branches on your mantel.

- **Angel Size:** Approximately 7 1/2" x 12"

- Scraps of 1 1/2"-wide Christmas prints
- 12" x 12" square cream print
- 3 1/2" x 3 1/2" square cream print
- All-purpose thread to match fabrics
- 1" wooden ball
- 2 yards 1/2"-wide cream ruffled lace
- 12" (3"-wide) wire-edged gold metallic ribbon
- 3" (3"-wide) wire-edged gold metallic ribbon
- 15" braided gold/red/green tinsel ribbon
- 8" (1/4"-wide) gold ribbon
- 4" gold tinsel pipe cleaner
- Small bunch of Spanish moss
- Small bunch of dried white German statice flowers
- 4 small red ribbon roses
- Spray starch
- Hot-glue gun and glue
- Basic sewing supplies and tools

Crazy for Angels
Placement Diagram
Approximately 7 1/2" x 12"

from one end to the other. *The block should look like a crazy Log Cabin when finished. No two blocks should look the same.*

Figure 1
Sew a strip to 1 side of the cream square.

Figure 2
Trim strips even with previous edge as shown.

Step 2. When pieced section is approximately 15" x 15", trim to 12" x 12". Stitch cream ruffled lace around edge of square raw edges even, easing at corners and overlapping ends on one side.

Figure 3
Block is shown after lace has been stitched.

Instructions

Step 1. Stitch a 1 1/2"-wide scrap strip to part of one side of the 3 1/2" x 3 1/2" cream print square; trim even with square as shown in Figure 1. Continue adding strips or various shapes to sides of the square, pressing and trimming after each addition as shown in Figure 2. **Note:** *The strips may be varying widths*

Step 3. Iron and heavily spray starch the 12" cream print square. Place right sides together with crazy-pieced block. Sew the pieces together, leaving a 3" opening on one side. Trim corners and any bulky areas on seam. Turn right side out through opening; hand-stitch opening closed; press as shown in Figure 3.

Step 4. Topstitch close to outside edges of stitched piece. Place on a flat surface with printed side down. Using a pencil, place a small dot in the center of the square. Place a small bead of hot glue on top of 1" round wooden ball. Place the ball on the center dot; let set to dry.

Step 5. Mold the fabric square around the wooden bead to form the head. Place the 15" piece of braided gold/red/green tinsel around bottom of wooden bead to form head. Tie in a knot and then form a bow, trimming ends if necessary.

Step 6. Play with the square a little to shape into a dress and two arm sections on each side, referring to the Placement Diagram.

Step 7. Form a bow from the 12" piece of 3"-wide wire-edged gold ribbon, bringing each end to the center of the ribbon section; hot-glue ends in place and let dry. Scrunch the center of the ribbon together to form bow. Fold the 3" piece of 3"-wide wire-edge gold ribbon into thirds and attach to center piece section of the bow, placing the wrong side of the center piece on the right side of the bow center; hot-glue in place for wings.

Step 8. Fold the 8" piece of gold ribbon in half to make a 4" loop. Hot-glue ends of this loop to the wrong side of the center section of wings. Set aside wings to be attached later.

Step 9. Roll a bunch of Spanish moss in your hand until it forms a little ball. Form this ball into a nest-like shape for hair. Fill with hot glue and place the Spanish moss hair on top of the head piece.

Step 10. Twist ends of gold tinsel pipe cleaner to form a small gold halo ring. Hot-glue small sprigs of dried white German statice flowers all around the outside of the halo. Hot-glue and evenly space four small red ribbon roses on the outside of the halo. Hot-glue the finished halo to the top of the Spanish moss hair.

Step 11. Attach the wings to back of angel by placing hot glue on the wrong side of the center section of the wings. Glue wings to backside base of the head.

Step 12. Play with the wings to make them fluff out. Hang angel on a tree, in an archway or over a door. ●

Home for Christmas

ecorating your home for Christmas is so much fun! Have fun stitching pillows for the sofa, pot holders for the kitchen, place mats for the table and a card holder to hang on the wall and display your greeting cards. You'll find pieced and appliquéd table toppers that can be used in any room. There's nothing like a touch of quilting to add warmth and cheer to a room!

Pine Tree Pillow

By Phyllis Dobbs

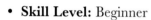

Select seasonal buttons and Christmas fabrics to make this creatve little accent pillow.

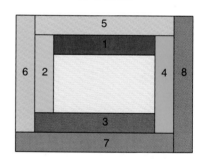

Pine Tree Pillow
Placement Diagram
14" x 10 1/2"

- **Skill Level:** Beginner
- **Project Size:** 14" x 10 1/2"
- **Block Size:** 14" x 10 1/2"
- **Number of Blocks:** 1

- 2"-wide scrap strips red and green fabrics
- 5" x 8 1/2" rectangle tan check
- 2 green print scraps
- Backing 11" x 14 1/2"
- Green all-purpose thread
- 10 round buttons in a variety of sizes and colors
- Snowflake and Christmas tree brass charms
- Christmas tree, Santa Claus, snowman and 3 star ceramic buttons
- 1 skein red 6-strand embroidery floss
- 4" x 9" piece iron-on adhesive
- Polyester fiberfill
- Basic sewing supplies and tools

Figure 2
Add strips to center rectangle
in numerical order as shown.

Instructions

Step 1. Cut one 2"-wide strip each in the following sizes and colors: 8 1/2" red for strip 1; 6 1/2" green for strip 2; 10" red for strip 3; 8" green for strip 4; 11 1/2" green for strip 5; 9 1/2" green for strip 6; 13" green for strip 7; and 11" red for strip 8.

Step 2. Sew strip 1 to 5" x 8 1/2" tan check rectangle as shown in Figure 1. Continue adding strips in numerical order referring to Figure 2; press seams toward strip after sewing each strip.

Figure 1
Sew strip 1 to
center rectangle.

Step 3. Prepare template for tree shape using pattern given on page 68. Trace three tree shapes onto paper side of iron-on adhesive; cut out shapes, leaving a margin beyond traced line.

Step 4. Fuse two shapes to the wrong side of one green scrap and one shape to the wrong side of a second green scrap. Cut shapes on traced lines; remove paper backing.

Step 5. Arrange tree shapes on the tan check area of the pieced block, with matching trees on the ends. Machine-appliqué shapes in place using green all-purpose thread.

Step 6. Using 3 strands red embroidery floss, stitch a row of running stitches 1/8" from seam inside tan check

Continued on page 68

Patched Cathedral Window

By Patsy Moreland

Use the jewel tones pictured or holiday scraps to make this pretty bellpull for your door. It's equally attractive hanging in a window or on a wall.

- **Skill Level:** Intermediate
- **Banner Size:** Approximately 11 1/2" x 20"

- 1/8 yard each 2 contrasting fabrics
- 1 1/8 yards background fabric
- Coordinating all-purpose thread
- 2 (2 1/4") coordinating tassels
- Basic sewing supplies and tools, No. 8 embroidery needle, knitting needle and 18" ruler with 60-degree-angle mark

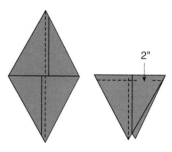

Figure 1
Fold background as shown. Pin pattern
piece to folded square; cut out.

square as shown in Figure 1; press.

Step 3. Pin pattern piece to folded square; cut out, being careful not to cut on fold lines, as shown in Figure 1; repeat for four pieces.

Step 4. Fold one piece in half right sides together; stitch ends as shown in Figure 2. Lay flat in diamond shape with stitched seams down the center; carefully press seams in opposite directions without pressing outer edges of diamond shapes. Fold in half across unstitched center of diamond with unseamed sides together; pin raw edges with right sides together and stitch center seam, leaving a 2" opening for turning as shown in Figure 3, being careful not to stitch back of diamond shape into seam. Press center seam open without pressing outer edges of diamond shape. Repeat for four pieces.

Figure 2
Stitch ends as shown.

Figure 3
Stitch center seam, leaving a 2" opening.

Step 5. Turn fabric to right side through unstitched 2" opening. Use knitting needle to push inside fabric points to stitching lines; hand-stitch opening closed. Repeat for four pieces; press.

Step 6. Pin fabric points in to the center; stitch all points of two rectangles and three points of the remaining two rectangles as shown in Figure 4.

Step 7. Pin two like units with folded sides together; slipstitch along long folded edge. Repeat with remaining two like units. Join the two pieced units together as shown in Figure 5.

Figure 4
Stitch all points of 2
rectangles and 3 points of
2 rectangles as shown.

Patched Cathedral Window
Placement Diagram
Approximately 11 1/2" x 20"

Instructions

Step 1. Prepare template using pattern piece given.

Step 2. Measure and cut background fabric into four 18" x 18" squares. Right sides together, fold each square in half, then in half again to make a 9" x 9"

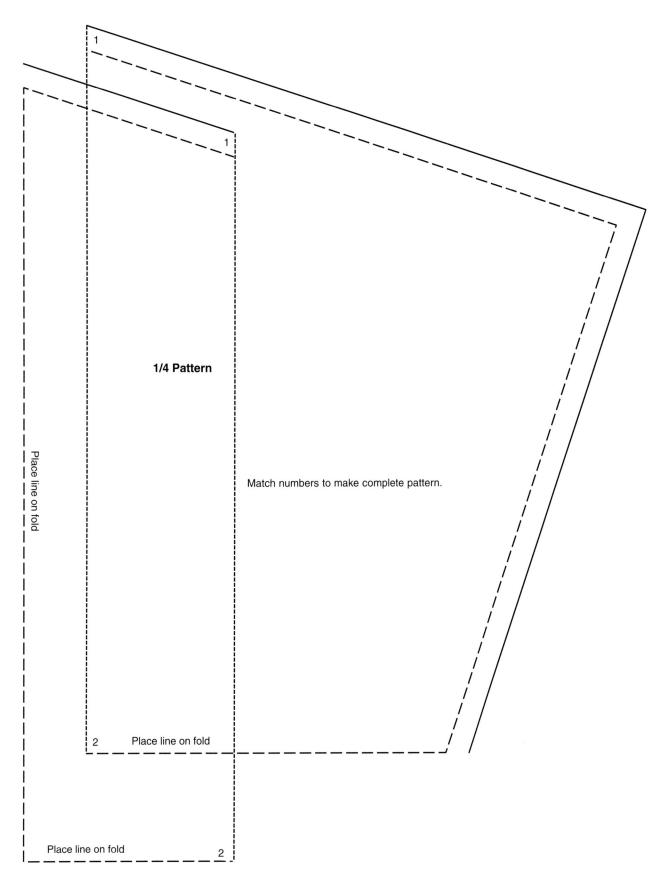

1/4 Pattern

Match numbers to make complete pattern.

Place line on fold

Place line on fold

Place line on fold

1

1

2

2

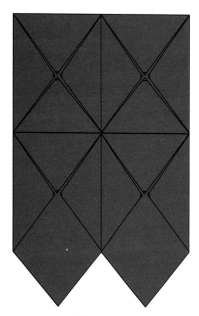

Figure 5
Join the units as shown.

Step 8. Hand-stitch a tassel at the bottom of each point using embroidery needle.

Step 9. Cut 1/8 yard fabrics into three each 1 5/8" x 22 1/2" strips; designate fabric 1 and fabric 2.

Step 10. Join two strips fabric 1 with one strip fabric 2 right sides together, staggering ends, as shown in Figure 6. Repeat with two strips fabric 2 and one strip fabric 1. Press seams in one direction.

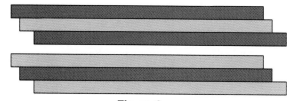

Figure 6
Join strips, staggering ends as shown.

Step 11. Align 60-degree ruler marking on right side of fabric strip at the seam. Cut the extended ends off. Measure 1 5/8" perpendicular from the cut line to make next cut; repeat for six segments from each set as shown in Figure 7.

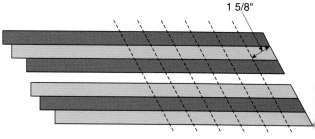

1 5/8"

Figure 7
Cut 1 5/8" segments from each angled strip.

Figure 8
Join segments to make 2 different diamond sets.

Step 12. Join three segments to make a diamond set, making two different diamond sets as shown in Figure 8; repeat for two diamond units of each set.

Step 13. Pin one diamond set inside each of the four center folded diamonds as shown in Figure 9. Roll edge of background over edge of diamond set as shown in Figure 10; slipstitch fabric folded edge in place, catching the diamond raw edge. Do not stitch through two backing layers. Repeat on each side of each diamond set.

Step 14. Add a fabric sleeve to backside referring to General Instructions to finish. ❧

Figure 9
Pin a diamond set inside each of 4 folded diamonds.

Figure 10
Roll folded edge over diamond set.

Dresden in the Round

By Meredith Yoder

over a round accent table with this pretty Dresden Plate-design tablecloth made in holiday prints. It's so easy you'll want to make them to give as gifts.

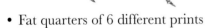

- **Skill Level:** Intermediate
- **Tablecloth Size:** 47" diameter
- **Number of Fan Units:** 12

- Fat quarters of 6 different prints
- Fat quarter red print
- 1 yard muslin
- 1 1/4 yards Christmas print
- Neutral color all-purpose thread
- 1 spool clear nylon monofilament
- Basic sewing supplies and tools

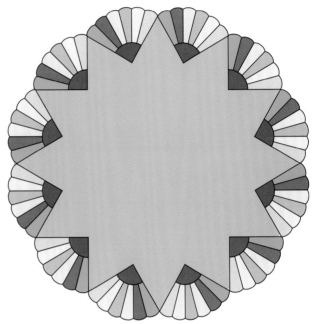

Dresden in the Round
Placement Diagram
47" diameter

Instructions

Step 1. Prepare templates using pattern pieces given. Cut as directed on each piece.

Step 2. Cut a 44" circle from the Christmas print referring to Figure 1 for cutting.

Step 3. Choose one A piece of each of the six different prints. Arrange in desired order as shown in Figure 2. Join two units; repeat for three units. Join units to complete one fan shape; press seams in one

direction. Repeat for 12 identical fans.

Step 4. Set piece B into pieced A units to complete fan units.

Step 5. Using pieced fan unit as a pattern, cut 12 muslin.

Step 6. Lay a muslin piece right sides together with a fan unit. Stitch all around outside edges; clip corners. Cut a hole through muslin layer *only* behind piece B on fan unit. Turn right side out through hole; press. Repeat for 12 lined fan units.

Step 7. Zigzag around outer edge of Christmas print circle using clear nylon monofilament.

Step 8. Divide circle in quarters; pin three fan units in each quarter, matching edge of fan unit with edge of circle as shown in Figure 3.

Figure 1
Fold and cut fabric to make a 44" circle.

Figure 2
Arrange A units as shown.

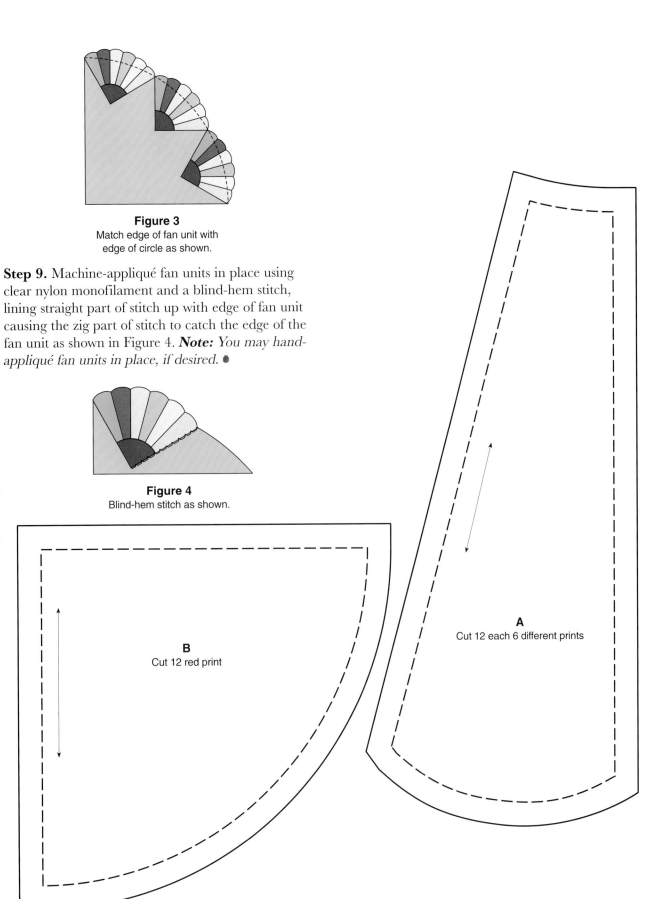

Figure 3
Match edge of fan unit with
edge of circle as shown.

Step 9. Machine-appliqué fan units in place using
clear nylon monofilament and a blind-hem stitch,
lining straight part of stitch up with edge of fan unit
causing the zig part of stitch to catch the edge of the
fan unit as shown in Figure 4. **Note:** *You may hand-
appliqué fan units in place, if desired.* ●

Figure 4
Blind-hem stitch as shown.

B
Cut 12 red print

A
Cut 12 each 6 different prints

Quick & Easy Christmas Strips

By Wendy Kinzler

I f you really want to make something quick, try these strip-pieced place mats. This same technique can be used for place mats of any shape.

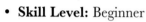

- **Skill Level:** Beginner
- **Place Mat Size:** 18" x 12"

- A variety of at least 12 strips ranging in width from 1 1/4" to 2" seasonal prints
- Backing 19" x 13"
- Batting 19" x 13"
- 1 3/4 yards self-made or purchased binding
- Neutral color all-purpose thread
- Permanent fabric pen
- Basic sewing supplies and tools

Quick & Easy Christmas Strips
Placement Diagram
18" x 12"

Quick & Easy Christmas Strips
Placement Diagram
18" x 12"

Instructions

Step 1. Mark a dot 4 1/2" from top right corner and 4 1/2" from bottom left corner on the piece of batting using permanent fabric pen. Connect the dots to make a diagonal line as shown in Figure 1.

Step 2. Draw horizontal and diagonal parallel lines on opposite sides of the diagonal line as shown in

Figure 2. Use these lines as guides for keeping strips straight when stitching.

Step 3. Place backing piece right side down on flat surface; lay marked batting piece on top marked side up.

Step 4. Arrange fabric strips for horizontal area in a pleasing order on a flat surface. Designating the first

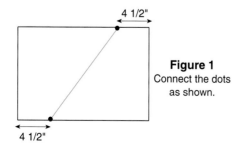

Figure 1
Connect the dots
as shown.

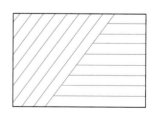

Figure 2
Draw lines as guides.

Figure 3
Pin strip A on batting.

Figure 4
Stitch through strips,
batting and backing.

strip as A, pin strip A on batting as shown in Figure 3; place strip B right sides together with A. Stitch along edge through batting, backing and strips as shown in Figure 4; press strip B down. Trim excess strip 1/2" from diagonal line.

Step 5. Continue adding strips until horizontal area of the batting piece is covered. Trim strips even with batting and backing.

Step 6. Arrange fabric strips for diagonal side and stitch referring to steps 4 and 5.

Step 7. Make a rectangle paper pattern 12" x 18"; place on stitched layers and trim even. ***Note:*** *The 12" x 18" rectangle may be made into an oval shape by folding paper pattern in quarters and cutting corners round. Place paper pattern on top of stitched layers; trim excess to match paper pattern.*

Step 8. Bind edges using self-made or purchased binding referring to General Instructions to finish. ▮

Holly Bells Pot Holders

By Marian Shenk

Decorate your kitchen with festive pot holders to bring holiday cheer to the chef!

Instructions

Step 1. Prepare templates for appliqué shapes. Cut as directed on each piece for one pot holder, adding a 1/4" seam allowance all around when cutting for hand appliqué. Repeat for second pot holder.

Step 2. Cut two squares each 8 1/2" x 8 1/2" red dot, cotton batting and green print.

Step 3. Fold one red dot square in half and in half again. Cut a round corner on folded square as shown in Figure 1. Use this square as a pattern to round corners on remaining fabric and batting squares.

Step 4. Arrange appliqué shapes on one red dot square referring to the Placement Diagram and photo for positioning of pieces; pin in place.

Step 5. Using coordinating all-purpose thread, hand-appliqué pieces in place in numerical order as shown in Figure 2.

Project Note

Materials listed will make two pot holders.

- **Skill Level:** Beginner
- **Pot Holder Size:** 8 1/2" x 8 1/2"

- 1/4 yard red dot
- 1/4 yard green print
- Scraps gold, red and green for appliqué
- 1/4 yard cotton batting
- Coordinating all-purpose thread
- White quilting thread
- Gold 6-strand embroidery floss
- 1 package green double-fold bias tape
- 2 (1") bone rings
- Basic sewing supplies and tools

Step 6. Using 3 strands gold embroidery floss, stem-stitch detail lines on bell and satin-stitch bell clappers.

Step 7. Sandwich a batting square between the appliquéd top and a green backing square. Pin layers together. Hand-quilt detail lines on leaves and around appliqué shapes using white quilting thread.

Step 8. Bind edges with green double-fold bias tape, overlapping ends. Turn binding to backside; hand-stitch in place.

Step 9. Hand-stitch a 1" bone ring to top corner to hang. Repeat for second pot holder.

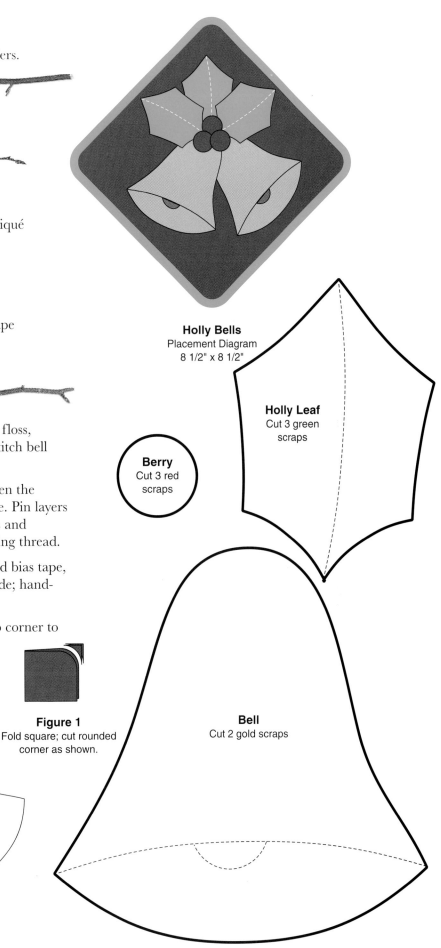

Holly Bells
Placement Diagram
8 1/2" x 8 1/2"

Holly Leaf
Cut 3 green
scraps

Berry
Cut 3 red
scraps

Bell
Cut 2 gold scraps

Figure 1
Fold square; cut rounded corner as shown.

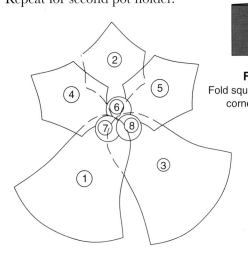

Figure 2
Hand-appliqué shapes in place
in numerical order as shown.

Wish Upon a Star

By Janice Loewenthal

Make a set of these place mats to give as gifts to special friends. This smiling angel will make any meal a time of joy and celebration.

Project Note

Materials listed will make two place mats.

Instructions

Step 1. Wash all fabrics; do not use fabric softener.

Step 2. Prepare templates using pattern pieces given.

Step 3. Cut blocks from the three coordinating fat quarters as follows: 6" x 9" for Tree block; 5 1/2" x 8 1/2" for Angel block; and 4" x 8 1/2" for Star block.

Step 4. Join blocks as shown in Figure 1 to make center for appliqué.

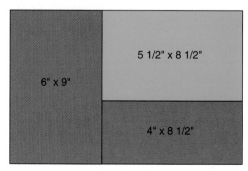

| 6" x 9" | 5 1/2" x 8 1/2" |
| | 4" x 8 1/2" |

Figure 1
Join blocks as shown.

Step 5. Trace each appliqué shape as directed for number to cut on the paper side of the fusible

Wish Upon a Star
Placement Diagram
Approximately 18 x 13"

- **Skill Level:** Beginner
- **Place Mat Size:** 18" x 13"

- 2/3 yard green quilted fabric
- 3 fat quarters coordinating fabrics
- Scraps green, red, white, gold, beige and tan for appliqué
- 1 package matching single-fold bias tape
- Coordinating all-purpose thread
- Gold metallic thread
- 1/2 yard fusible transfer web
- 40 assorted buttons
- Black permanent fabric pen
- Basic sewing supplies and tools

transfer web. Cut shapes apart leaving a margin around traced lines.

Step 6. Fuse shapes to fabrics as directed on each piece for color. Cut out shapes on traced lines; remove paper backing.

Step 7. Referring to patterns for order of appliqué, arrange tree shapes on the 6" x 9" rectangle, angel shapes on the 5 1/2" x 8 1/2" rectangle and star shapes on the 4" x 8 1/2" rectangle referring to the Placement Diagram and photo of project for positioning; fuse in place.

Step 8. Using coordinating all-purpose thread or gold metallic thread, satin-stitch around each shape in the same order as pieces were fused. Add angel's eyes,

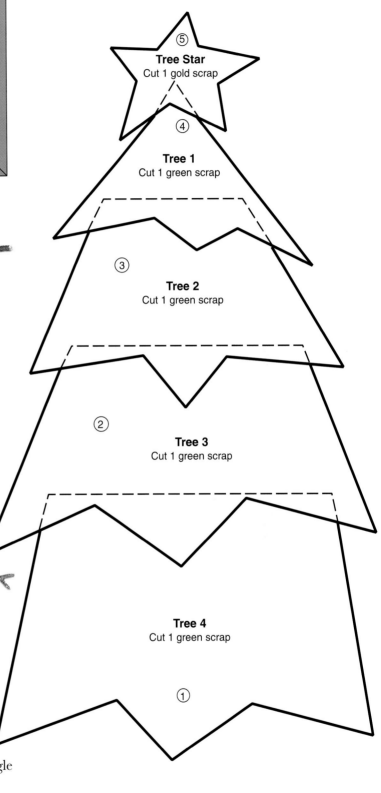

⑤

Tree Star
Cut 1 gold scrap

④

Tree 1
Cut 1 green scrap

③

Tree 2
Cut 1 green scrap

②

Tree 3
Cut 1 green scrap

Tree 4
Cut 1 green scrap

①

nose and mouth using black permanent fabric pen.

Step 9. Cut a piece of fusible transfer web 9" x 14" (same size as the pieced rectangle); place on wrong side of pieced and appliquéd center. Fuse in place; remove paper backing.

Step 10. Cut a piece of green quilted fabric 17" x 22". Center fused rectangle on top as shown in Figure 2; fuse in place.

Step 11. Place single-fold bias tape along one edge of green quilted rectangle with right sides together; stitch. Repeat for each side.

Step 12. Bring folded edge of binding over the raw edges of the pieced center block, mitering corners of binding and quilted backing as shown in Figure 3. Trim excess from under miters; hand- or machine-stitch binding in place.

Step 13. Sew assorted buttons to the border areas to finish. Repeat for second place mat. ❧

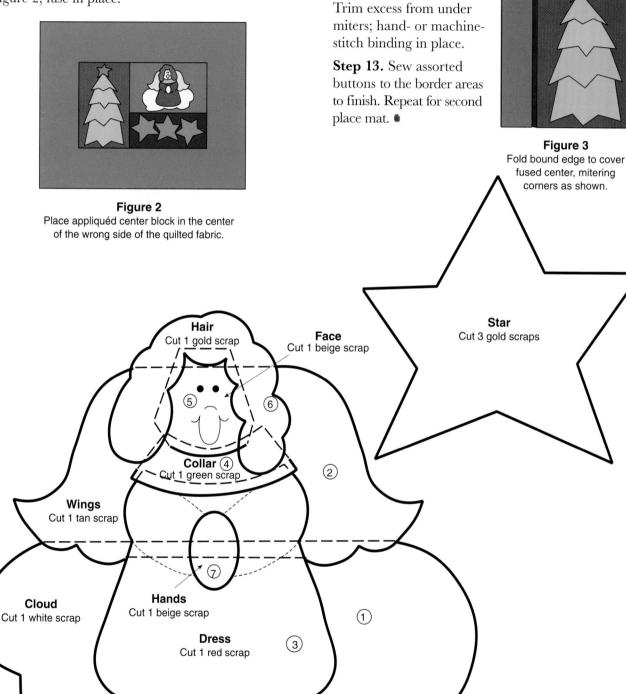

Figure 2
Place appliquéd center block in the center of the wrong side of the quilted fabric.

Figure 3
Fold bound edge to cover fused center, mitering corners as shown.

Hair
Cut 1 gold scrap

Face
Cut 1 beige scrap

Star
Cut 3 gold scraps

Collar ④
Cut 1 green scrap

Wings
Cut 1 tan scrap

Cloud
Cut 1 white scrap

Hands
Cut 1 beige scrap

Dress
Cut 1 red scrap

Countdown With Santa

By Kathy Brown

Put candy in Santa's pouch for a treat each day as you count the days until Christmas. For a special surprise, add several small Christmas presents.

Countdown With Santa
Placement Diagram
20" x 15"

Instructions

Step 1. Join six 3" x 3" squares as shown in Figure 1 referring to the project photo for placement of each fabric; repeat for second strip. Press seams in one direction. Sew a strip to the 15 1/2" sides of the blue-and-white print rectangle; press seams toward strips.

Step 2. Join six 3" x 3" squares in color order shown in Figure 2; repeat for second strip. Press seams in one direction. Sew a strip to the remaining sides of the blue-and-white print rectangle; press seams toward strips.

Step 3. Prepare appliqué templates using full-size patterns given. Trace

- **Skill Level:** Intermediate
- **Project Size:** 20" x 15"

Scraps white, red, black and tan fabrics
- Scraps cotton batting
- 4 squares red-and-green plaid 3" x 3"
- 6 squares each red stripe and green plaid 3" x 3"
- 8 squares gold print 3" x 3"
- 1 rectangle blue-and-white print 10 1/2" x 15 1/2"
- 1 rectangle green star print 6" x 12"
- Batting 24" x 19"
- Backing 24" x 19"
- Polyester fiberfill
- All-purpose thread to match fabrics
- 1/4 yard fusible transfer web
- Pre-made 1 1/2" white iron-on numbers
- Black permanent fabric pen
- 2 white 1/2" buttons
- Basic sewing supplies and tools

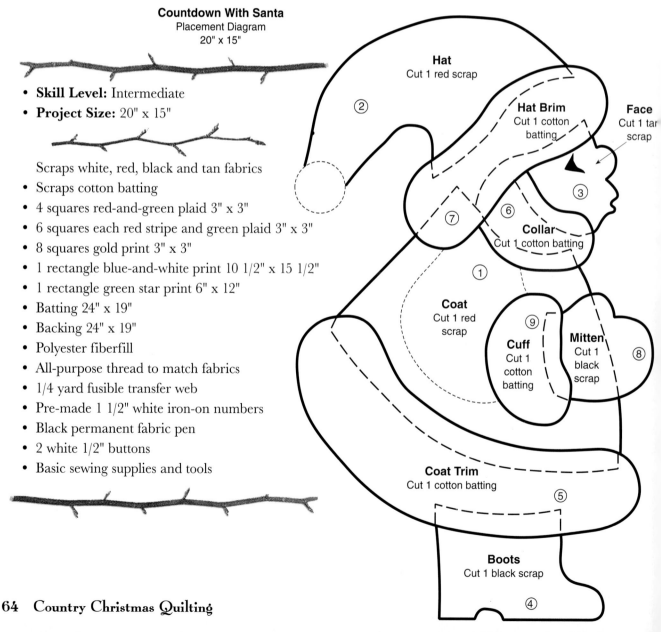

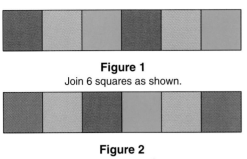

Figure 1
Join 6 squares as shown.

Figure 2
Join 6 squares as shown.

pieces onto paper side of fusible transfer web. Cut out shapes, leaving a margin beyond traced lines.

Step 4. Fuse cutout shapes to the wrong side of fabric and cotton batting scraps referring to pattern for color and number to cut. Cut out shapes on traced lines; remove paper backing.

Step 5. Arrange Santa, Mrs. Santa and heart shapes on blue-and-white print background in numerical order for each design referring to full-size patterns; fuse shapes in place. Add eyes to Santa and Mrs. Santa using black permanent fabric pen referring to patterns for placement.

Step 6. Place 24" x 19" piece of batting under pieced and appliquéd section; pin layers together. Machine-appliqué shapes in place with matching all-purpose thread through both layers. Satin-stitch sleeve lines as shown on pattern. Trim batting even.

Step 7. Fuse numbers in place on border squares referring to the Placement Diagram for positioning.

Step 8. Fold each 6" edge of the 6" x 12" rectangle green star print to inside 1/2"; stitch. Fold in half with right sides together; sew along side seams. Turn right side out. Hand-stitch top edges to mitten areas of appliquéd shapes, pleating on the underneath side to fit. Place a small amount of polyester fiberfill inside bag.

Step 9. Place backing piece right sides together with appliquéd top; stitch all around, leaving a 4" opening on one side. Turn right side out; hand-stitch opening closed.

Step 10. Sew a 1/2" white button to the end of each hat to finish. ●

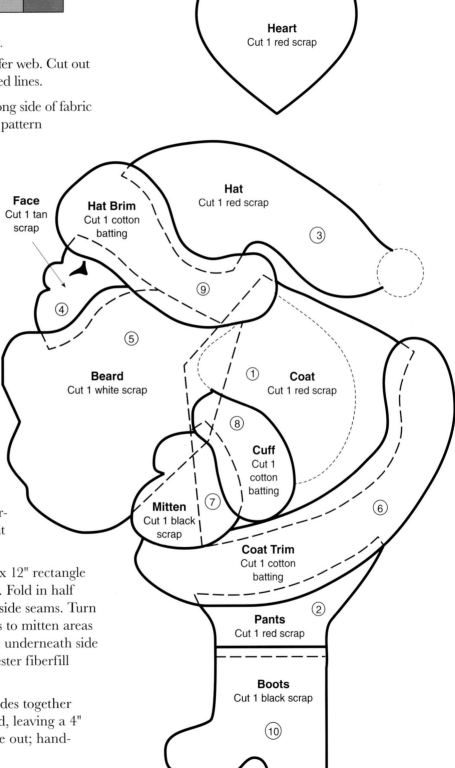

Heart
Cut 1 red scrap

Hat
Cut 1 red scrap

Face
Cut 1 tan scrap

Hat Brim
Cut 1 cotton batting

Beard
Cut 1 white scrap

Coat
Cut 1 red scrap

Cuff
Cut 1 cotton batting

Mitten
Cut 1 black scrap

Coat Trim
Cut 1 cotton batting

Pants
Cut 1 red scrap

Boots
Cut 1 black scrap

Pinwheel Patches

By Holly Daniels

The colors used to make this table topper give it a real country look. It would look great on a table or buffet or draped across a treasured wood chest or trunk.

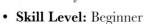

- **Skill Level:** Beginner
- **Project Size:** 44" x 14"
- **Block Size:** 10" x 10"
- **Number of Blocks:** 4

- 1/4 yard green print
- 1/4 yard light beige stripe
- 1/4 yard dark red print
- 1 1/4 yards tan stripe (lengthwise stripe used in project)
- Backing 48" x 18"
- Batting 48" x 18"
- 3 1/2 yards self-made or purchased binding
- Neutral color all-purpose thread
- Basic sewing supplies and tools

Instructions

Step 1. Cut three strips tan stripe 2 1/2" wide along length of fabric; set aside for borders.

Step 2. Prepare templates using pattern pieces given. Cut as directed on each piece. ***Note:** Place stripe line on template A along fabric stripe when cutting tan stripe and light beige stripe pieces. Use grainline arrow for template A placement when cutting dark red print pieces.*

Step 3. Sew a dark red print A triangle to a tan stripe A triangle; press seams toward darker fabric. Repeat for 16 units.

Step 4. Join four A units as shown in Figure 1; repeat for four units.

Figure 1
Join 4 A units.

Step 5. Cut one strip green print 4 3/8" by fabric width. Cut strip into 4 3/8" segments. Cut each segment in half on one diagonal to make B triangles. You will need 16 B triangles.

Step 6. Sew a B triangle to each side of one pieced A unit as shown in Figure 2; press seams toward B. Repeat for four units.

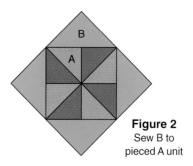

Figure 2
Sew B to
pieced A unit

Step 7. Sew an A triangle to each long side of C as shown in Figure 3; repeat for 16 units. Sew an A-C unit to each side of the previously pieced A-B unit as shown in Figure 4 to complete block; repeat for four blocks.

Figure 3
Sew A to C.

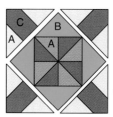

Figure 4
Join pieced units to
complete 1 block.

Step 8. Join the four pieced blocks to make one long strip; press.

Step 9. From tan stripe strips cut in Step 1, cut two strips each 2 1/2" x 40 1/2" and 2 1/2" x 10 1/2"; sew longer strips to long sides of block strip. Press seams toward strips.

Step 10. Cut four squares dark red print 2 1/2" x 2 1/2". Sew a square to each end of each 2 1/2" x 10 1/2" tan

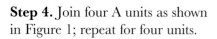

stripe strip. Sew a strip to remaining short ends of pieced unit; press seams toward strips.

Step 11. Prepare pieced top for quilting and finish referring to General Instructions. ▪

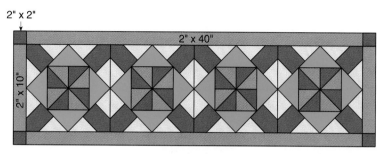

Pinwheel Patches
Placement Diagram
44" x 14"

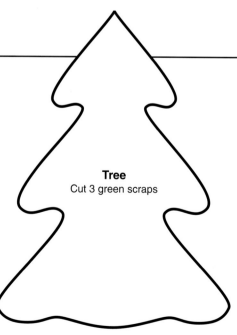

Pinwheel
10" x 10" Block

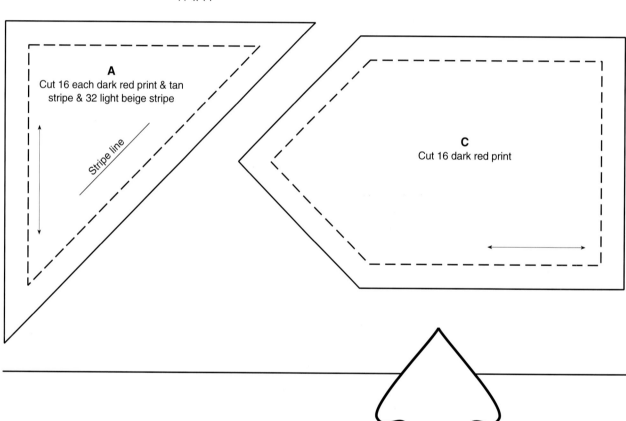

A
Cut 16 each dark red print & tan stripe & 32 light beige stripe

Stripe line

C
Cut 16 dark red print

Tree
Cut 3 green scraps

Pine Tree Pillow
continued from page 48

continued from page 48

center and 1/8" inside seam of first round of strips.

Step 7. Hand-stitch star buttons on top of trees; stitch remaining buttons in place referring to the photo for positioning suggestions.

Step 8. Place 11" x 14 1/2" backing piece right sides together with appliquéd block. Stitch around all sides leaving a 4" opening on one side. Turn right side out.

Step 9. Stuff pillow lightly with polyester fiberfill. Hand-stitch opening closed to finish. ▪

Pine Tree Greetings

By Jill Reber

S ort and store your Christmas cards in this cute and functional card holder this holiday season.

- **Skill Level:** Beginner
- **Project Size:** 8" x 28"

- Scraps green, brown, gold and tan prints
- 1/2 yard red print
- 3/4 yard plaid
- Backing 12" x 32"
- Batting 12" x 32"
- Neutral color all-purpose thread
- Natural linen thread
- 4 1/2" x 4 1/2" square fusible transfer web
- 1" brown button
- Basic sewing supplies and tools

Instructions

Step 1. Cut one square green print 5 1/4" x 5 1/4"; cut on both diagonals to make A triangles. You will need three A triangles.

Step 2. Cut three squares tan print 2 7/8" x 2 7/8"; cut each square in half on one diagonal to make B triangles. You will need six B triangles.

Step 3. Cut one rectangle brown print 1 1/2" x 2 1/2" for C.

Step 4. Cut two rectangles tan print 2 1/2" x 2" for D.

Step 5. Sew a B triangle to each short side of A as shown in Figure 1; repeat for three units. Join the three

Pine Tree Greetings
Placement Diagram
8" x 28"

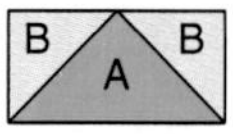

Figure 1
Sew B triangles
to A.

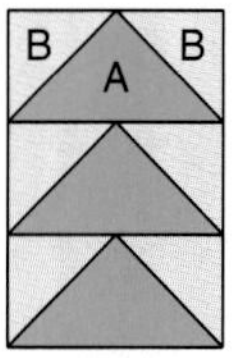

Figure 2
Join 3 units to
make tree top.

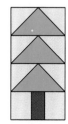

Figure 3
Sew D to C.

Figure 4
Join pieced units
to make a tree.

pieced units to complete tree top as shown in Figure 2.

Step 6. Sew D to each long side of C as shown in Figure 3. Join the A-B unit with the C-D unit to complete the tree unit as shown in Figure 4.

Step 7. Cut three rectangles red print 2 1/2" x 8 1/2". Sew a rectangle to opposite long sides of the pieced tree unit; press seams toward rectangles. Sew the remaining rectangle to the top of the pieced unit; press seams toward strips.

Step 8. Cut one rectangle plaid 8 1/2" x 18 1/2". Sew to the bottom of the tree unit; press.

Step 9. Cut three rectangles red print 2 1/2" x 8 1/2" and three rectangles plaid 5 1/2" x 8 1/2" for pockets.

Step 10. Press the three red print pieces in half along the 8 1/2" length with wrong sides together. Pin the raw edges of one folded piece to the right side of a plaid rectangle on the 8 1/2" side; stitch. Finish seam with serger or zigzag stitch; press seam toward plaid. Repeat for three pockets.

Step 11. Sandwich batting between the tree unit and prepared backing; pin or baste layers together.

Step 12. Pin one pocket 5 3/4" down from bottom of tree unit as shown in Figure 5; stitch across. Press pocket up; baste in place along sides. Repeat with second pocket 5 3/4" down from the first pocket; stitch across. Press pocket up.

Step 13. Pin the final pocket even with bottom edge of tree unit; baste in place.

Step 14. Stitch pockets in place along sides. Trim edge of backing and batting even with top unit edge.

Step 15. Machine-quilt around tree shapes and as desired.

Step 16. Prepare 3 yards red-print binding and bind edges referring to General Instructions.

Step 17. Cut two squares gold print 4 1/2" x 4 1/2". Bond the fusible transfer web square to the wrong side of one gold square; remove paper backing. Fuse the remaining gold square to the fused gold square.

Step 18. Prepare template for star shape; trace onto fused gold square. Cut out on traced line.

Step 19. Attach star to top of tree with linen thread and button, tying a knot on the top of the button and leaving several long loops of thread on the backside for hanging. ●

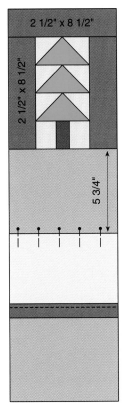

Figure 5
Pin 1 pocket 5 3/4"
down from bottom
of tree unit.

Star

Christmas in the Woods

By Marian Shenk

Turn your card table into a beautiful piece of furniture when you cover it with this pretty appliquéd and pieced quilt. Its crazy-patch trees and sleighs full of presents bring holiday cheer.

- **Skill Level:** Intermediate
- **Quilt Size:** 48" x 48"
- **Block Size:** 6" x 6"
- **Number of Blocks:** 16

- 1/8 yard each 6–8 green prints for trees
- 1/4 yard red print 1 for blocks
- 1/4 yard dark green solid wool for sleigh appliqués
- 1/2 yard muslin for crazy-patchwork foundation
- 1/2 yard red print 2 for blocks
- 1 yard white-on-white print for center background
- 4" x 6" scrap brown solid for tree trunks
- Scraps bright prints for packages
- 1 yard green print for blocks and inside border strips
- Backing 54" x 54"
- Batting 54" x 54"
- 6 yards self-made or purchased binding
- 1 yard each 5 colors of narrow ribbon to match packages to make bows
- 1 yard 1/4"-wide flat gold braid for sleigh runners
- 2 yards 1/8" gold cord for sleigh supports
- All-purpose thread to match fabrics
- 1 spool white quilting thread
- Basic sewing supplies and tools and wash-out marker or pencil

Instructions

Step 1. Cut a piece of white-on-white print 34 1/2" x 34 1/2" for background. Fold and crease to mark center lines.

Step 2. Prepare templates for appliqué pieces. Cut sleighs, packages and tree trunks as directed on each piece, adding a 1/8"–1/4" seam allowance when cutting. Turn under edges of each appliqué shape; baste in place.

Step 3. Cut four pieces muslin 10" x 13". Cover each piece with crazy-patchwork using 1/8-yard green print fabrics. Starting in the center, place a patch with a second patch on top; stitch across one raw edge.

Fold over top piece; press. Continue adding patches until muslin foundation is covered as shown Figure 1. Repeat for four foundation pieces. Place tree pattern on one crazy-patchwork piece; cut out, adding a 1/8"–1/4" seam allowance when cutting. Turn under edges; baste in place. Repeat for four trees.

Figure 1
Cover muslin foundation
with crazy patchwork.

Step 4. Pin a crazy-patchwork tree and trunk at each corner, placing trunk 3" away from corner. Hand-appliqué in place using matching thread.

Step 5. Cut two pieces of one color narrow ribbon, each 1/4" longer than the Ribbon Placement lines shown on one package pattern; cut one more piece 7" long for bow. Repeat for five packages, using a different ribbon for each package.

Step 6. Center and pin sleigh pieces at side centers, placing sleigh bottom 2" away from edge. Using thread to match fabrics, hand-appliqué package pieces in place inside sleigh in numerical order according to pattern, slipping ribbon ends under edges before stitching down as shown in Figure 2. Make a bow for each package; hand-stitch in place. Appliqué sleigh piece in place after all packages have been stitched.

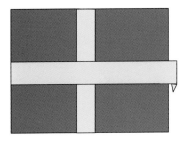

Figure 2
Slip ribbon ends for wrapping under edge
of package before stitching down.

Step 7. Cut a 16" piece of gold cording. Transfer runner support design to background under sleigh using wash-out marker or pencil. Hand-stitch cording along marked line, stitching through underside of

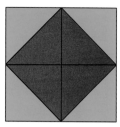

Triangle Block 1
6" x 6"
Make 4

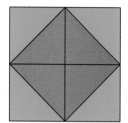

Triangle Block 2
6" x 6"
Make 12

Christmas in the Woods
Placement Diagram
48" x 48"

Figure 5
Join 3 side units to
make 1 border strip.

cording. Repeat for four sleighs.

Step 8. Cut a 7 1/4" piece flat gold braid for runner. Hand-stitch in place under gold cording for runner. Repeat for four sleighs.

Step 9. Prepare template for A; cut as directed on the A piece. Sew a green print A to a red print A; repeat for all A triangles. Press seams to one side.

Step 10. Join four A-A red print 1 units as shown in Figure 3 to make Triangle Block 1; repeat for four

blocks. Join four A-A red print 2 units, again referring to Figure 3, to make Triangle Block 2; repeat for 12 blocks.

Step 11. Join four A-A red print 1 units with a Triangle Block 1 as shown in Figure 4 to make a side unit; repeat for four side units. Join four A-A red print 2 units with a Triangle Block 2 as shown in Figure 4 to make a side unit 2; repeat for eight side unit 2s.

Step 12. Join two side unit 2s with one side unit 1 as shown in Figure 5 to make border strips; repeat for four border strips.

Step 13. Cut two strips green print 1 1/2" x 34 1/2"; sew to opposite sides of appliquéd center. Press seams toward strips.

Step 14. Cut two strips green print 1 1/2" x 36 1/2"; sew to remaining sides of appliquéd center. Press seams toward strips.

Figure 3
Join 4 A-A units to make block.

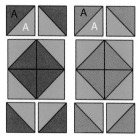

Figure 4
Join 4 A-A units with Triangle
blocks to make side units.

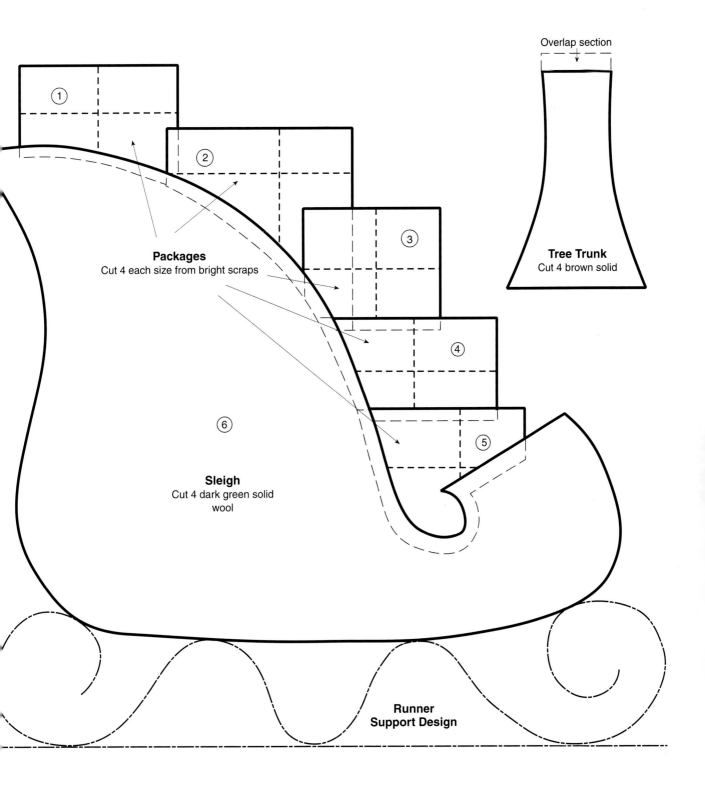

Overlap section

① ② ③ ④ ⑤ ⑥

Packages
Cut 4 each size from bright scraps

Tree Trunk
Cut 4 brown solid

Sleigh
Cut 4 dark green solid
wool

**Runner
Support Design**

Step 15. Sew a pieced border strip to opposite sides of center; press seams toward strips. Sew a Triangle Block 2 to each end of the remaining two border strips. Sew a strip to the remaining sides of center; press seams toward strips.

Step 16. Prepare quilt for quilting and finish as in General Instructions, binding edges with self-made or purchased binding. ●

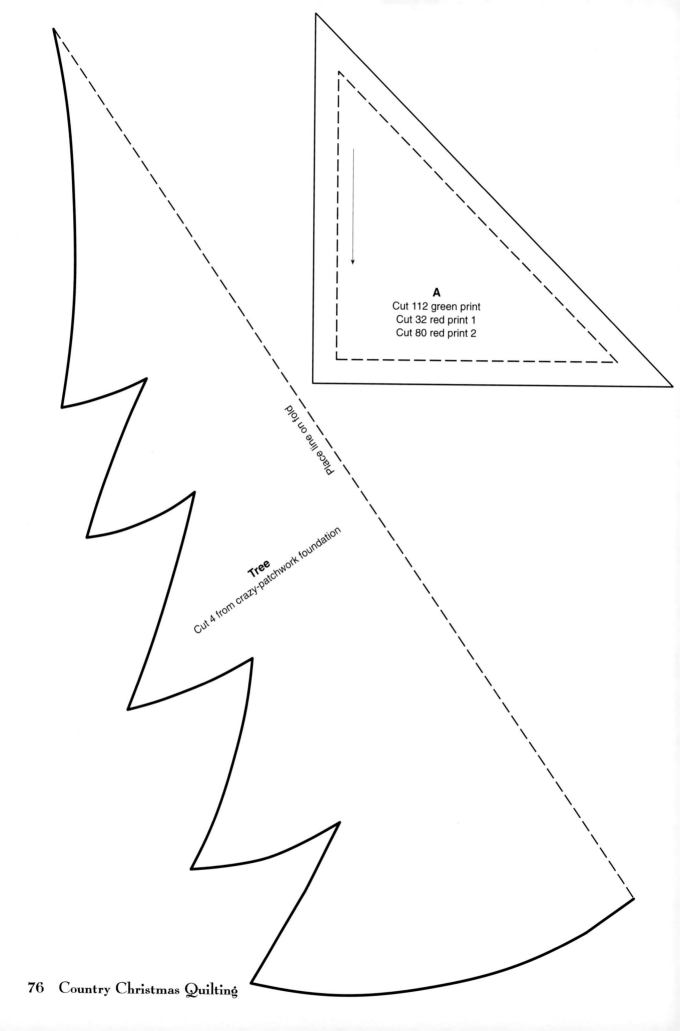

A
Cut 112 green print
Cut 32 red print 1
Cut 80 red print 2

Place line on fold

Tree
Cut 4 from crazy-patchwork foundation

Anthurium Wreath Pillow

By Charlyne Stewart

I've had many opportunities to admire the Hawaiian influence on California homes. The anthurium is a popular design motif. The colors of this project make it appropriate for an added accent to any room during the holidays.

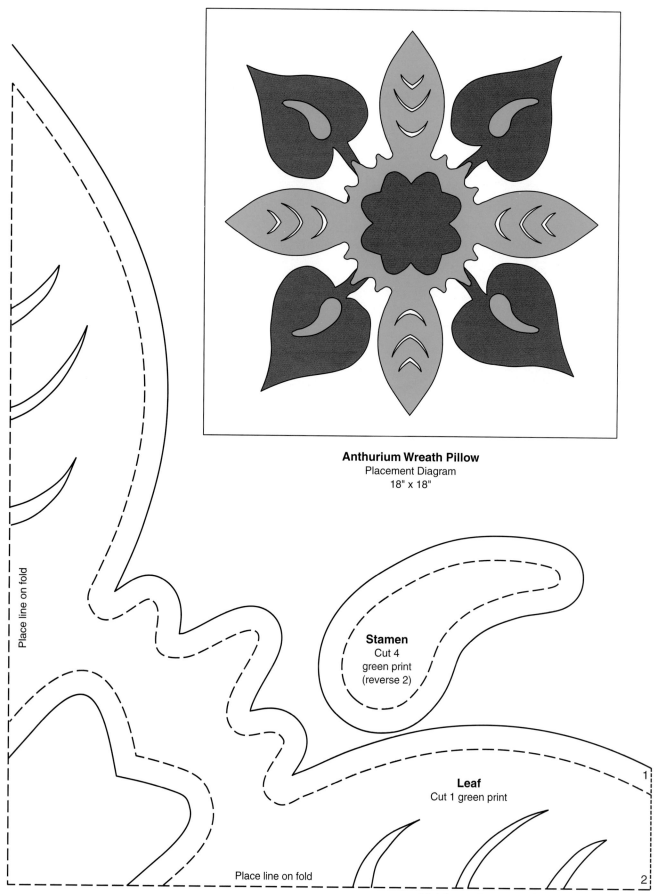

Anthurium Wreath Pillow
Placement Diagram
18" x 18"

Place line on fold

Stamen
Cut 4
green print
(reverse 2)

1

Leaf
Cut 1 green print

Place line on fold

2

Match numbers to make complete pattern

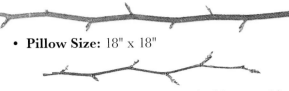

- **Pillow Size:** 18" x 18"

- 5/8 yard each green print and white-on-white print
- 1 yard red solid
- Batting 20" x 20"
- 18" x 18" pillow form
- All-purpose thread to match fabrics
- 1 spool white quilting thread
- 2 1/2 yards 1/4"-wide cable cord
- 1 package each snowflake sequins and small green seed beads
- Basic sewing supplies and tools and cardboard

Project Notes

Traditional and reverse appliqué techniques were used to complete this pillow. The red center shape is placed under the green leaf, then the leaf is appliquéd over the center. The leaf-slits are cut out to reveal the background; the slits are turned under and stitched down. The remaining pieces use traditional appliqué with edges turned under and pieces stitched to the background.

INSTRUCTIONS

Step 1. Prewash all fabrics. Prepare templates for each pattern piece. Cut as directed on each piece.

Step 2. Cut two 19" x 19" squares white-on-white print for background and backing. Fold one square into eight equal sections as shown in Figure 1; press after each fold.

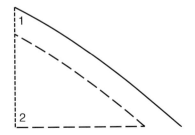

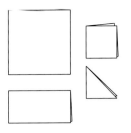

Figure 1
Fold background square as shown.

Step 3. Cut a 5 1/2" x 5 1/2" square red solid. Fold and crease on the diagonal to find center. Align corners on center creases of the background as shown in Figure 2.

Figure 2
Place red square on
background as shown.

Step 4. Referring to Figure 3, cut out center shapes on leaf section using solid lines on pattern as guides for cutting. Pin the green print cut-out on the background over the red square aligning each leaf point with the center background creases; baste in place.

Figure 3
Cut out shapes for
reverse appliqué.

Step 5. Pin a flower shape in between leaf shapes aligning each flower point with a diagonal background crease and referring to the Placement Diagram for positioning. Tuck stem end under leaf section; baste in place.

Step 6. Turn edges of leaf-slit sections under to reveal white background. Hand-stitch edges down. Turn edges under all around on leaf and petal shapes. Hand-appliqué shapes in place.

Step 7. Pin a stamen shape on each petal; hand-appliqué in place.

Step 8. Sandwich batting between appliquéd top and the 19" x 19" white-on-white backing piece. Baste layers together to hold.

Step 9. Hand- or machine-quilt around edges of

shapes, in cut-out areas and as desired on background piece.

Step 10. When quilting is complete trim edges even. Sew snowflake sequins in a random pattern in the background areas. Sew a green seed bead in the center of each snowflake sequin.

Step 11. Cut and piece a 1 1/4" x 90" strip of bias from the red solid. Fold strip over cording piece. Stitch cording inside bias strip, sewing close to cord as shown in Figure 4. *Note: A zipper foot would help make this step easier.*

Figure 4
Sew bias strip over cord, stitching close to cord.

Step 12. Stitch cording to pillow top as shown in Figure 5, clipping at corners and folding in raw edges on one end over the other, butting cording as shown in Figure 6.

Figure 5
Stitch piping
to pillow top.

Step 13. Cut one square red solid 19" x 19". Place right sides together with completed pillow top. Stitch all around sides using a 1/2" seam allowance and leaving a 6" opening on one side.

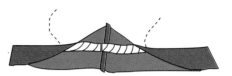

Figure 6
Butt ends of cord.

Step 14. Turn right side out through opening. Insert pillow form; hand-stitch opening closed to finish. ●

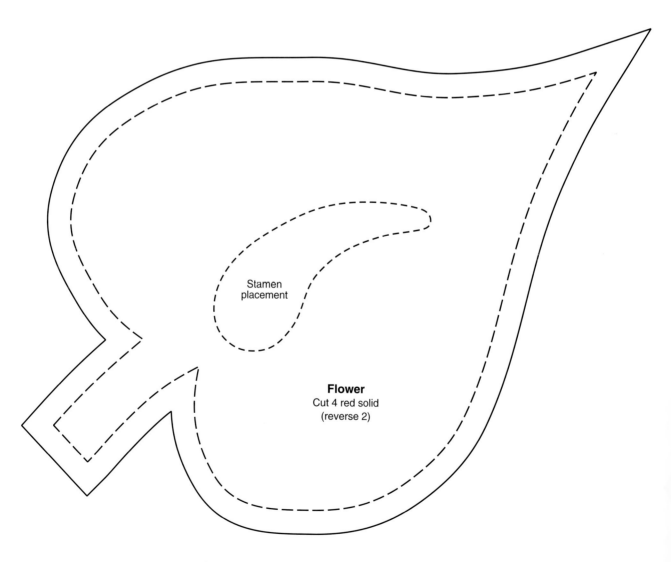

Stamen
placement

Flower
Cut 4 red solid
(reverse 2)

Dining in the Pines

By Charlyne Stewart

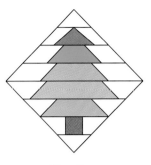

Pine Tree
10" x 10" Block

The pine tree is a favorite design to use for Christmas projects. Although there are many templates, this is an easy design to piece.

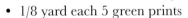

- **Skill Level:** Beginner
- **Project Size:** 42 3/8" x 14 1/8"
- **Block Size:** 10" x 10"
- **Number of Blocks:** 3

- 1/8 yard each 5 green prints
- 1/2 yard white-metallic print
- 1/2 yard green-metallic print
- Scrap gold print
- Backing 45" x 15"
- Batting 45" x 15"
- 1 spool white all-purpose thread
- 1 spool each white and green quilting thread
- Basic sewing supplies and tools

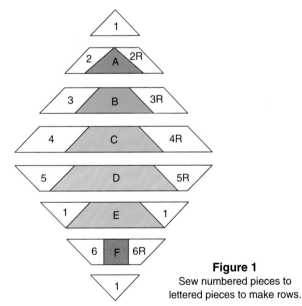

Dining on the Pines
Placement Diagram
42 3/8" x 14 1/8"

Figure 1
Sew numbered pieces to lettered pieces to make rows.

Instructions

Step 1. Assign a number to each of the five green prints. Prepare templates using pattern pieces given. Cut as directed on each piece for one block; repeat for three blocks.

Step 2. To piece one block, sew numbered pieces to lettered pieces to make rows referring to Figure 1.

Step 3. Join rows as shown in Figure 2; add piece 1 to top and bottom to complete one block. Repeat for three blocks.

Step 4. Cut one square green metallic print 15 3/8" x 15 3/8". Cut on both diagonals to make four triangles.

Step 5. Sew triangles to squares as shown in Figure 3 to make diagonal rows; press seams toward triangles.

Step 6. Join diagonal rows to complete pieced top.

Step 7. Place pieced top on backing and batting pieces; cut to same size as pieced top. Place batting piece on flat surface; lay backing on top right side up. Place pieced top right sides together with backing piece.

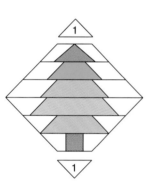

Figure 2
Join rows as shown; add
piece 1 to top and bottom.

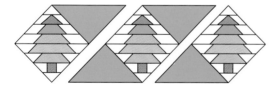

Figure 3
Join blocks with triangles in diagonal rows.

Step 8. Stitch around all sides leaving a 6" opening on one side. Clip corners; turn right side out. Press flat; hand-stitch opening closed.

Step 9. Mark quilting design in triangles referring to General Instructions.

Step 10. Quilt on marked lines using green quilting thread. Quilt blocks around tree shapes using white quilting thread to finish. 🍂

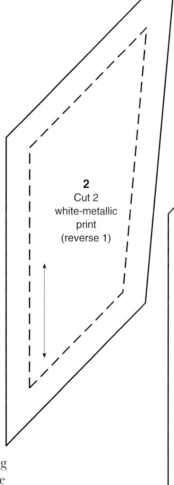

2
Cut 2
white-metallic
print
(reverse 1)

3
Cut 2 white-metallic print
(reverse 1)

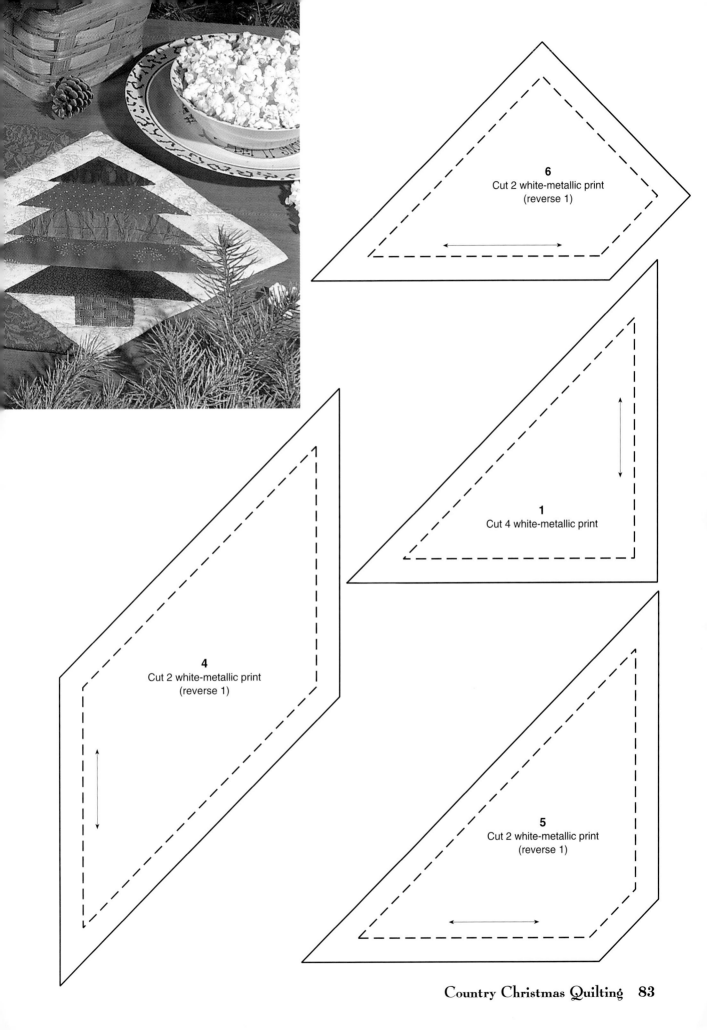

6
Cut 2 white-metallic print
(reverse 1)

1
Cut 4 white-metallic print

4
Cut 2 white-metallic print
(reverse 1)

5
Cut 2 white-metallic print
(reverse 1)

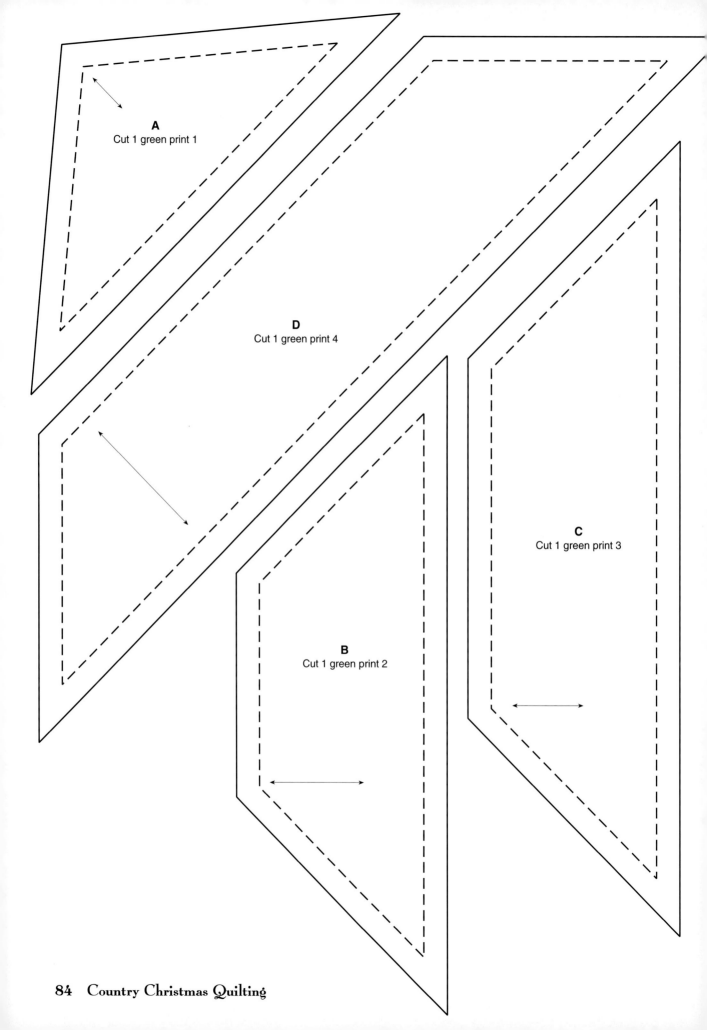

A
Cut 1 green print 1

D
Cut 1 green print 4

C
Cut 1 green print 3

B
Cut 1 green print 2

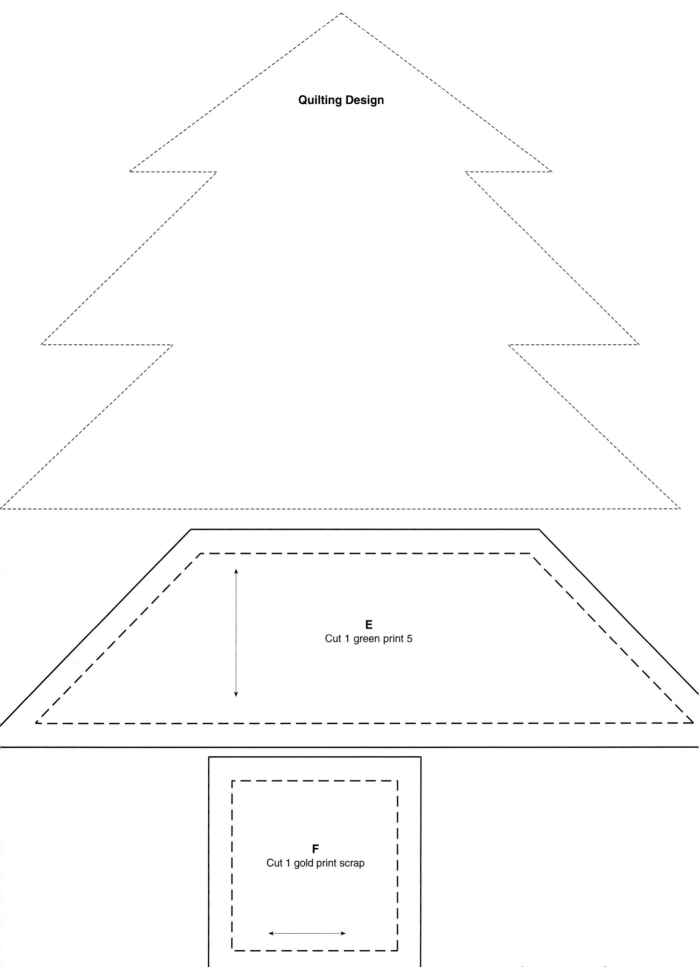

Quilting Design

E
Cut 1 green print 5

F
Cut 1 gold print scrap

Christmas Finery

Add sparkle and pizzazz to your wardrobe with Christmas aprons, jackets and jumpers. You'll find fun ties for Dad and Grandpa, snazzy sweatshirts for kids and a fashionable denim shirt design for teens. Of course, there are lots of projects to make for yourself or as gifts for your quilting friends. Step out in style this Christmas season wearing quilted clothing that's fun and easy to make.

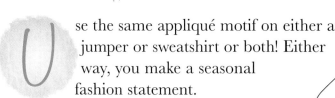

Spice on Ice

By Kathy Brown

Use the same appliqué motif on either a jumper or sweatshirt or both! Either way, you make a seasonal fashion statement.

Sweatshirt

- **Skill Level:** Beginner
- **Sweatshirt Size:** Adult

- Cream adult sweatshirt
- Scrap fabric for appliqué as follows: burgundy, green, brown, gold and assorted prints and gold solid
- All-purpose thread to match fabrics
- 1/2 yard fusible transfer web
- 5/8 yard tear-off fabric stabilizer
- 14 (4mm) black beads
- Basic sewing supplies and tools

Instructions

Step 1. Wash all fabrics and sweatshirt; do not use fabric softener.

Step 2. Prepare templates for each appliqué shape using pattern pieces given. Trace shapes onto paper side of fusible transfer web. Cut out each shape leaving a margin around traced lines.

Step 3. Fuse shapes to fabric scraps referring to patterns for color suggestions and number to cut. Cut shapes on traced lines; remove paper backing.

Step 4. Arrange appliqué motifs and stars on sweatshirt front referring to the Placement Diagram and photo of project for positioning. Fuse shapes in place.

Step 5. Cut a piece of tear-off fabric stabilizer larger than area behind fused shapes; pin to the backside of the sweatshirt front. Using matching all-purpose

Spice on Ice Sweatshirt
Placement Diagram
Adult Size

thread, machine-appliqué shapes in place using a machine satin stitch. Remove fabric stabilizer.

Step 6. Sew 4mm black beads to gingerbread men and skate placket referring to pattern for placement.

Jumper

- **Skill Level:** Beginner
- **Jumper Size:** Adult

- Commercial pattern for jumper with bodice
- Fabric and notions as listed on pattern
- Scrap fabric for appliqué as follows: burgundy, green, brown, gold and assorted prints and gold solid
- All-purpose thread to match fabrics
- 1/2 yard fusible transfer web
- 5/8 yard tear-off fabric stabilizer
- 4 (4mm) black beads
- 10 (1/4") black buttons with shanks
- Basic sewing supplies and tools

Instructions

Step 1. Wash all fabrics; do not use fabric softener.

Step 2. Cut jumper pieces using commercial pattern.

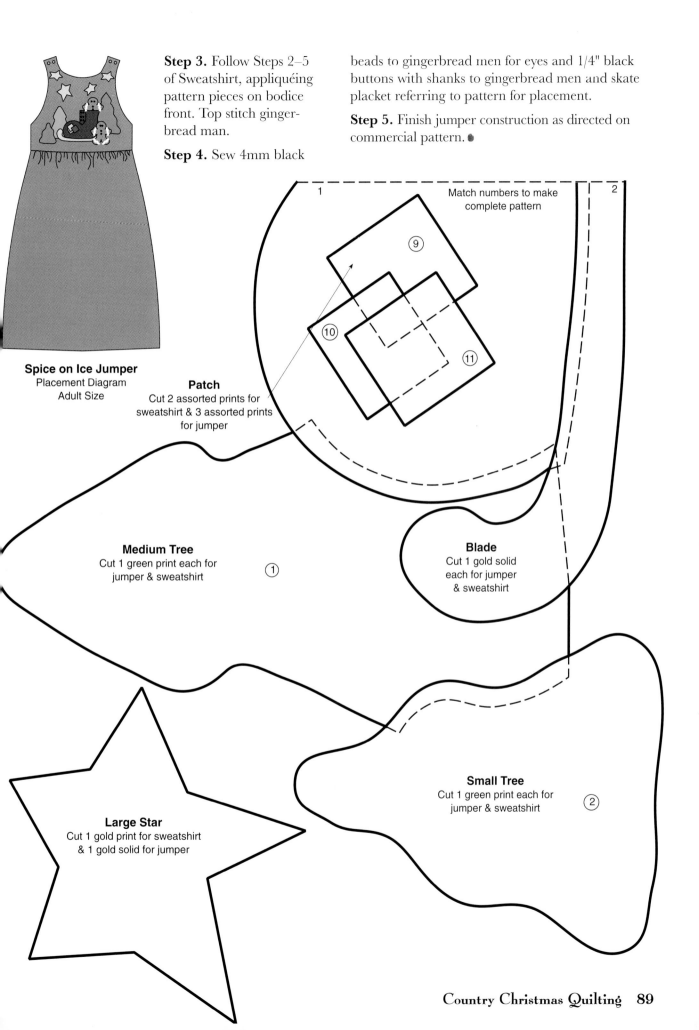

Step 3. Follow Steps 2–5 of Sweatshirt, appliquéing pattern pieces on bodice front. Top stitch gingerbread man.

Step 4. Sew 4mm black beads to gingerbread men for eyes and 1/4" black buttons with shanks to gingerbread men and skate placket referring to pattern for placement.

Step 5. Finish jumper construction as directed on commercial pattern. ●

Spice on Ice Jumper
Placement Diagram
Adult Size

1   Match numbers to make complete pattern   2

⑨

⑩

⑪

Patch
Cut 2 assorted prints for
sweatshirt & 3 assorted prints
for jumper

Medium Tree
Cut 1 green print each for
jumper & sweatshirt
①

Blade
Cut 1 gold solid
each for jumper
& sweatshirt

Small Tree
Cut 1 green print each for
jumper & sweatshirt
②

Large Star
Cut 1 gold print for sweatshirt
& 1 gold solid for jumper

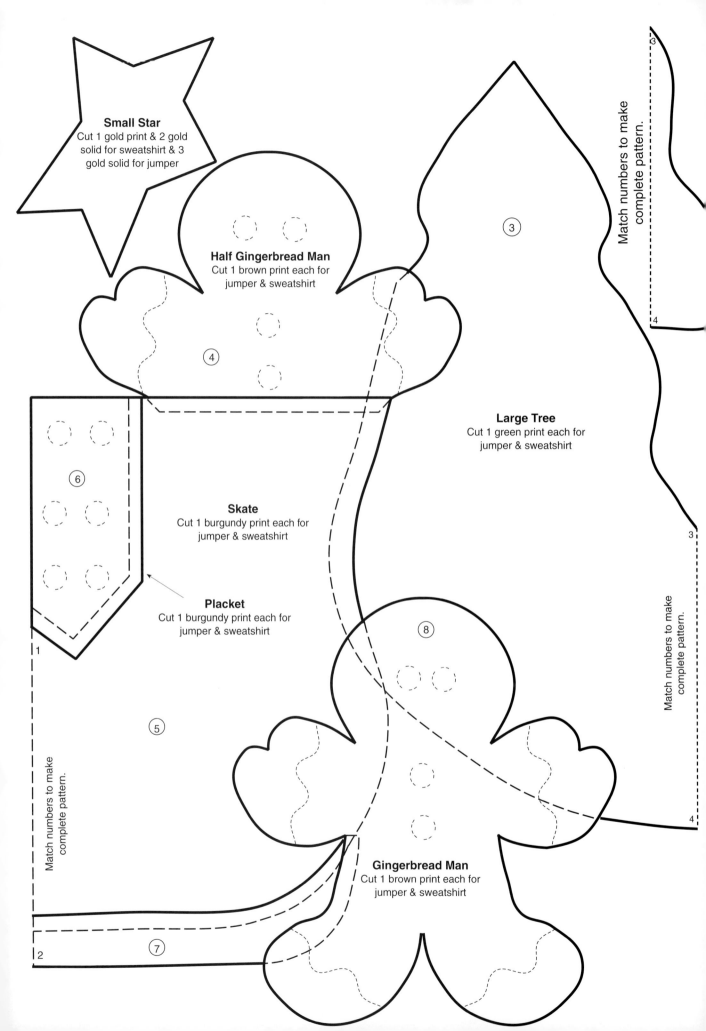

Small Star
Cut 1 gold print & 2 gold
solid for sweatshirt & 3
gold solid for jumper

Half Gingerbread Man
Cut 1 brown print each for
jumper & sweatshirt

3

Large Tree
Cut 1 green print each for
jumper & sweatshirt

Match numbers to make
complete pattern.

4

4

Skate
Cut 1 burgundy print each for
jumper & sweatshirt

6

Placket
Cut 1 burgundy print each for
jumper & sweatshirt

1

5

8

3

Match numbers to make
complete pattern.

Match numbers to make
complete pattern.

4

Gingerbread Man
Cut 1 brown print each for
jumper & sweatshirt

2

7

Snow Folks Jumper

By Kathy Brown

Dress up a simple jumper with some quick appliqué for your holiday parties. This smiling trio of snowmen with three-dimensional scarfs will help you celebrate the holidays in style.

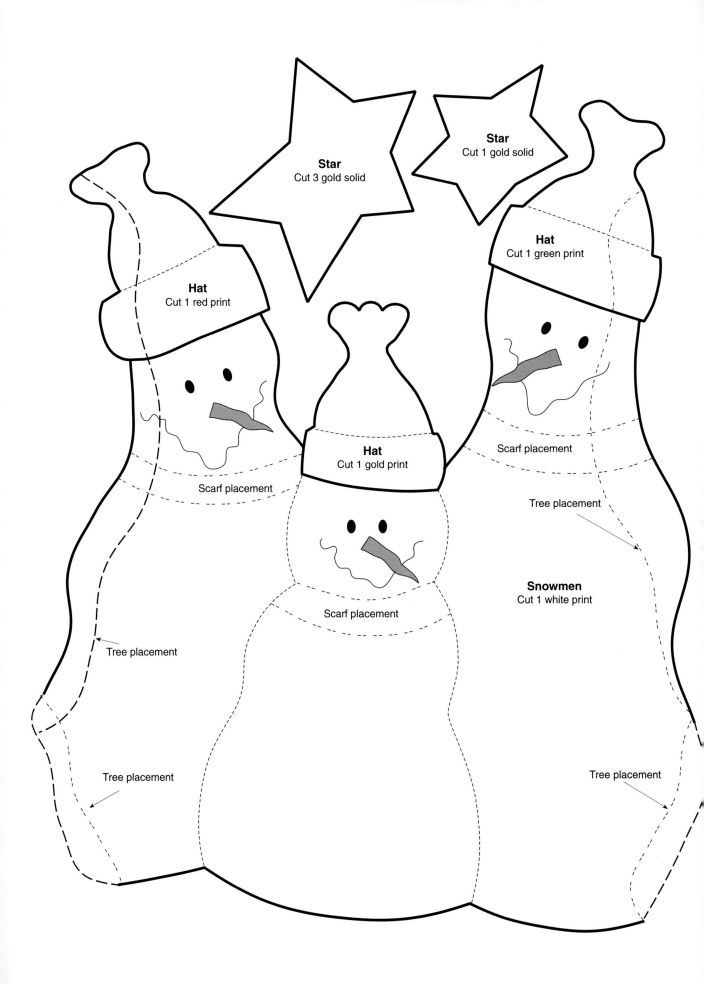

Star
Cut 3 gold solid

Star
Cut 1 gold solid

Hat
Cut 1 green print

Hat
Cut 1 red print

Hat
Cut 1 gold print

Scarf placement

Scarf placement

Scarf placement

Tree placement

Snowmen
Cut 1 white print

Tree placement

Tree placement

Tree placement

Snow Folks Jumper
Placement Diagram
Adult Size

- **Skill Level:** Beginner
- **Jumper Size:** Adult

- Jumper pattern with bodice top
- Fabric and notions for jumper as listed
  on pattern
- Scrap fabric for appliqué as follows: red, white,
  green and gold prints and gold solid
- Orange and black all-purpose thread
- 1/2 yard fusible transfer web
- 1/2 yard tear-off fabric stabilizer
- .05 black permanent fabric pen
- Basic sewing supplies and tools

Instructions

Step 1. Wash all fabrics; do not use fabric softener.

Step 2. Prepare templates for each appliqué shape using pattern pieces given. Trace shapes onto paper side of fusible transfer web. Cut out each shape leaving a margin around traced lines.

Step 3. Fuse shapes to fabric scraps referring to patterns for color suggestions and number to cut. Cut shapes on traced lines; remove paper backing.

Step 4. Cut jumper pieces using purchased pattern. Mark center front of bodice piece.

Step 5. Arrange appliqué motifs and stars in numerical order on the bodice center front referring to Figure 1, the Placement Diagram and photo of project for positioning. Fuse shapes in place.

Step 6. Cut a piece of tear-off fabric stabilizer larger than area behind fused shapes; pin to the backside of the bodice front. Using black all-purpose thread, machine-appliqué shapes in place using a machine featherstitch. Using orange all-purpose thread, zigzag nose shapes on all three snowmen. Remove fabric stabilizer. Using the .05 black permanent fabric pen, make eyes and mouths.

Step 7. Tear three strips from scrap fabrics 3/4" x 16". Hand-stitch each end of one strip to each snowman for scarf, as marked on pattern for positioning. Cut strips in the center; tie in a bow to finish.

Step 8. Finish jumper construction as directed on commercial pattern. ●

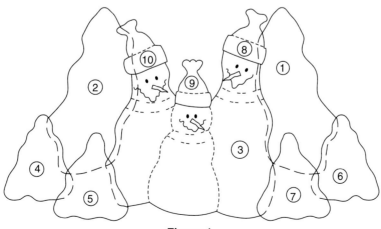

Figure 1
Arrange pieces on bodice front in numerical order as shown.

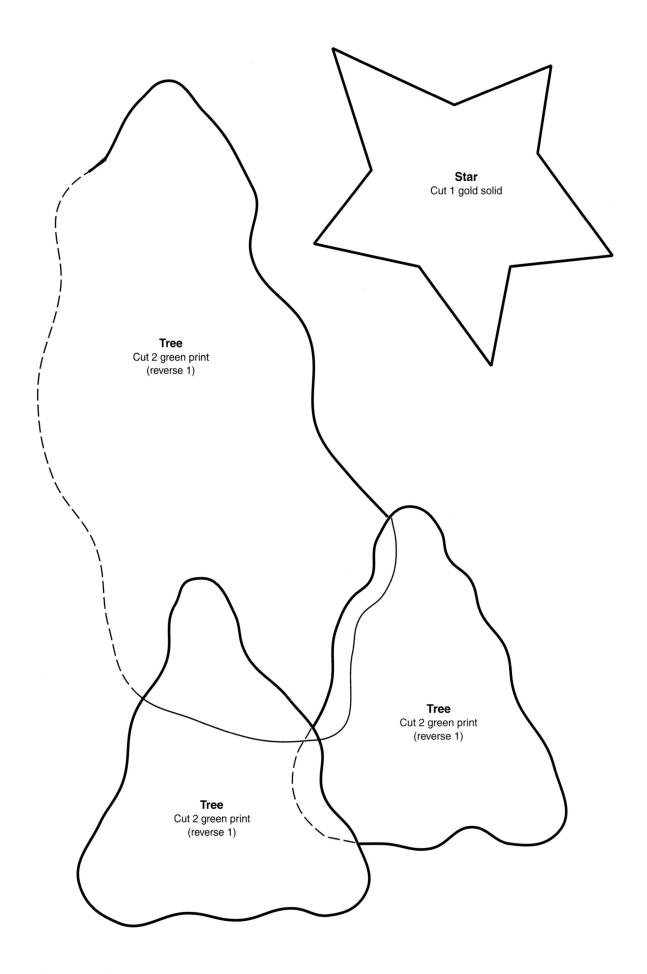

Star
Cut 1 gold solid

Tree
Cut 2 green print
(reverse 1)

Tree
Cut 2 green print
(reverse 1)

Tree
Cut 2 green print
(reverse 1)

Snuggles the Snowbuddy

By Kathy Brown

Even in jeans and a denim shirt, you can be dressed up for the season. Make this friendly snowman with his three-dimensional stocking cap a part of your winter wardrobe.

- **Skill Level:** Beginner
- **Shirt Size:** Adult

- Adult-size denim shirt
- 6" x 5" piece red check flannel
- Scrap fabric for appliqué as follows: 2 green prints, gold print and gold and black solids
- 6" x 10" piece cotton batting
- 1 red ribbed sock
- Orange, red, off-white, gold and black all-purpose thread
- 3/8 yard fusible transfer web
- 1/4 yard tear-off fabric stabilizer
- 2 (2mm) black beads
- Basic sewing supplies and tools

Instructions

Step 1. Wash all fabrics; do not use fabric softener.

Step 2. Prepare templates for each appliqué shape using pattern pieces given. Trace shapes onto paper side of fusible transfer web. Cut out each shape leaving a margin around traced lines.

Step 3. Fuse shapes to fabric scraps referring to patterns for color suggestions and number to cut. Cut shapes on traced lines; remove paper backing.

Step 4. Arrange snowman appliqué motifs on right shirt front and stars on left shirt front referring to the Placement Diagram and photo of project for positioning. Fuse shapes in place.

Step 5. Cut 3" off the ribbed part of the sock for hat; set aside. To make socks, cut 1/2" more off the ribbed part of the sock; cut this piece into two identical strips referring to sock placement on pattern for guide to size. Pin in place at top of boots.

Step 6. Cut a piece of tear-off fabric stabilizer larger than area behind fused shapes; pin to the backside of the shirt front. Using matching all-purpose thread, machine-appliqué shapes in place using a machine satin stitch. Using orange all-purpose thread, zigzag nose shape on snowman. Using black all-purpose thread, zigzag mouth. Remove fabric stabilizer.

Step 7. Cut a 1/2" x 6" strip gold print. Turn up

Snuggles the Snowbuddy
Placement Diagram
Adult Size

one end of 3" section of sock ribbing about 1/2"; tack in place. Pinch the other end together; tie off with gold print strip to make the hat. Hand-stitch to top of snowman's head. Trim gold print strip to desired length.

Step 8. Tear one strip gold print 3/4" x 8". Hand-stitch each end of strip to snowman neck for scarf, as marked on pattern for positioning. Cut strip in the center; tie in a knot; trim to desired length to finish.

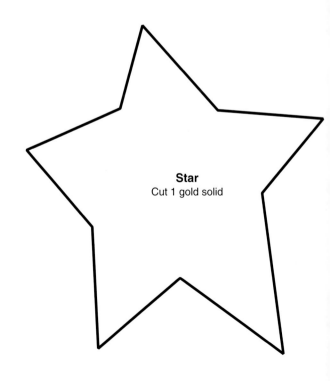

Star
Cut 1 gold solid

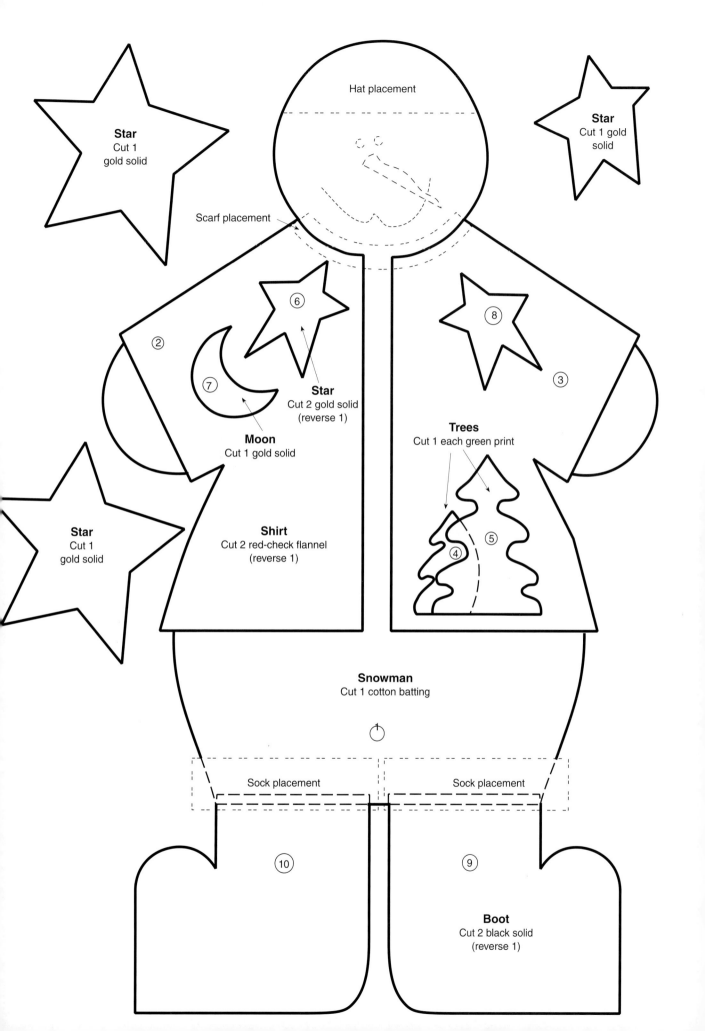

Star
Cut 1
gold solid

Star
Cut 1 gold
solid

Hat placement

Scarf placement

②

⑥

⑦

⑧

③

Star
Cut 2 gold solid
(reverse 1)

Moon
Cut 1 gold solid

Star
Cut 1
gold solid

Trees
Cut 1 each green print

④

⑤

Shirt
Cut 2 red-check flannel
(reverse 1)

Snowman
Cut 1 cotton batting

Sock placement

Sock placement

⑩

⑨

Boot
Cut 2 black solid
(reverse 1)

Holly
Sweatshirt Jacket

By Ann Boyce

Stay warm and comfortable wearing this sweatshirt jacket. Its cascade of holly leaves and berries will add a festive flavor to your day.

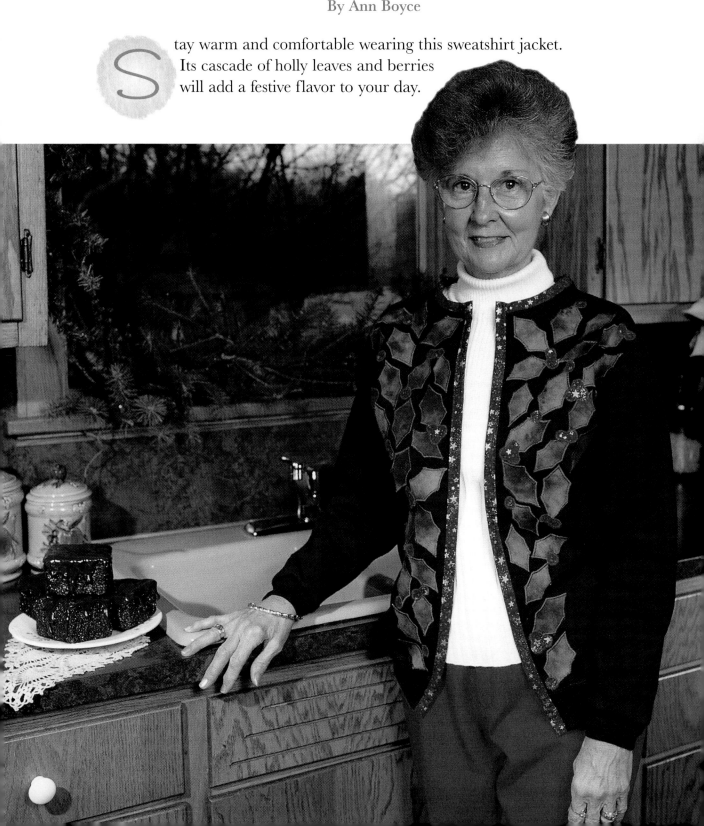

- **Skill Level:** Beginner
- **Jacket Size:** Adult

- Adult-size black sweatshirt
- 1 fat quarter green mottled
- 1/2 yard red print
- 1 spool each red and green all-purpose thread
- 1/2 yard fusible transfer web
- Basic sewing supplies and tools

Holly Sweatshirt Jacket
Placement Diagram
Adult Size

Instructions

Step 1. Cut one rectangle each green mottled and fusible transfer web 11" x 18". Apply fusible transfer web to wrong side of fabric rectangle.

Step 2. Cut one rectangle each red print and fusible transfer web 6" x 12". Apply fusible transfer web to wrong side of fabric rectangle.

Step 3. Prepare template for holly and berry shapes. Trace onto paper side of fused fabrics as directed on pattern pieces for color and number to cut. Cut out on traced lines; remove paper backing. Set aside.

Step 4. Mark and cut center front of sweatshirt from top to bottom. Cut off 1/2" neckline ribbing.

Step 5. Prepare 1 yard red print 2"-wide bias binding and bind neck edge referring to General Instructions.

Step 6. Measure center front line; cut two strips red print 2" by this measurement. Turn under one long raw edge of each strip 1/4"; press. Using a 1/2" seam allowance, sew a strip to one center front edge with right side of binding strip together with wrong side of sweatshirt edge.

Step 7. Turn binding strip to right side of sweatshirt; topstitch in place close to folded edge. Repeat for

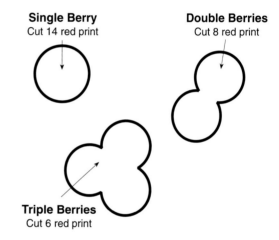

Single Berry
Cut 14 red print

Double Berries
Cut 8 red print

Triple Berries
Cut 6 red print

both center front edges.

Step 8. Pin and fuse 23 large and small holly leaves along each sweatshirt front. Repeat with seven single, four double and three triple berries on leaves as desired.

Step 9. Machine-appliqué each leaf and berry shape in place using all-purpose thread to match fabrics.

Large Holly Leaf
Cut 20 green mottled

Small Holly Leaf
Cut 26 green mottled

Happy Gingerbread

By Janice Loewenthal

Use the same appliqué motifs on two very different projects to create a coordinated Christmas wardrobe.

Happy Gingerbread Apron
Placement Diagram
Adult Size

Apron

Skill Level: Beginner

• **Apron Size:** Adult

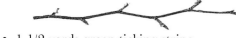

• 1 1/2 yards green ticking stripe
• Scrap fabric for appliqué as follows: red/white/green stripe, green dot and red, green and tan prints
• Batting 12" x 12"
• White all-purpose thread
• All-purpose thread to match fabrics
• 1/4 yard fusible transfer web
• 1/4 yard tear-off fabric stabilizer
• 1 package red rickrack
• 4 (1/2") red buttons
• 5 (5/8") red buttons
• .05 black permanent fabric pen
• Makeup blusher
• White acrylic paint
• Basic sewing supplies and tools and toothpick

Instructions

Step 1. Wash all fabrics; do not use fabric softener.

Step 2. To make apron cut green ticking stripe

pieces as follows: 22" x 36" for skirt; two pieces 6" across fabric width for waistband/ties; two 4" x 22" strips following stripes for neck ties; two pieces 7" x 8" with stripes running parallel to 7" edge for pockets; and two 12" x 12" squares for bib.

Step 3. Turn under 1/4" along one 7" edge (top) of pocket; stitch. Fold over top edge 1" right sides together; stitch ends referring to Figure 1. Turn right side out. Turn under 1/4" on remaining three sides; press. Cut a piece of red rickrack 20" long; stitch rickrack on these three sides. Repeat for second pocket.

Figure 1
Stitch ends as shown.

Step 4. Place batting under one 12" x 12" square green ticking stripe for bib front; pin or baste to hold layers together.

Step 5. Prepare templates for each appliqué shape using pattern pieces given. Trace shapes onto paper side of fusible transfer web. Cut out each shape leaving a margin around traced lines.

Step 6. Fuse shapes to fabric scraps referring to patterns for color suggestions and number to cut. Cut shapes on traced lines; remove paper backing.

Step 7. Arrange candy cane shapes with holly leaves on pocket and gingerbread boy/girl, leaves and bow on bib front referring to the Placement Diagram and photo of project for positioning. Fuse shapes in place.

Step 8. Cut a piece of tear-off fabric stabilizer larger than area behind fused shapes; pin to the backside of the pocket and bib front. Using thread to match fabrics, machine-appliqué shapes in place. Using white all-purpose thread, make a decorative scallop stitch on each gingerbread boy/girl arm. Remove fabric stabilizer. Using the .05 black permanent fabric pen, make eyes, mouths and noses. Add a dot of white acrylic paint with toothpick to eyes for highlight. Use makeup blusher to add cheek color.

Step 9. Stitch two 1/2" red buttons to each pocket and five 5/8" red buttons to bib front referring to the Placement Diagram and project photo for positioning.

Step 10. Fold each 4" x 22" strip green ticking stripe in half along length with right sides together. Stitch along length and diagonally across one end. Turn right side out; press. Pin the open end of one strip 1/2" from the side edge of the top corner of the bib front with pointed end of strip facing center front as shown in Figure 2; repeat for second strip on remaining top corner.

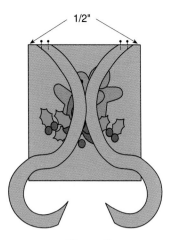

Figure 2
Pin strip to bib front as shown.

Step 11. Place remaining 12" x 12" square green ticking stripe right sides together with bib front. Stitch around two sides and across top, leaving bottom edge open. Turn right side out; press.

Step 12. Cut a piece of red rickrack 34" long. Sew rickrack around two sides and across top of lined bib front. Mark center at bottom of bib front.

Step 13. Sew the 6" by fabric width strips green ticking stripe together on one short end to make one long strip. Measure and mark 9" on each side of the seam. Fold strip in half along length with right sides together. Sew diagonally across ends and along length to the marks. Turn right side out; press. Press under 1/4" on one raw edge between marks for waistband/tie.

Step 14. To make skirt, press under a double 1/4" seam on two 22" sides and on one 36" edge for bottom; stitch to hem. Mark the center of the 36" raw edge; sew a row of gathering stitches 1/4"–1/2" from top edge. Pull gathering thread to make an 18" skirt top.

Step 15. Pin bottom of bib front to top of skirt, matching center fronts as shown in Figure 3. Place raw edge of open area of layered waistband/tie piece onto the apron. ***Note:*** *The open area on waistband/tie should match the size of the gathered skirt piece.* Stitch seam.

Step 16. Fold remaining layer of waistband/tie over to cover seam; hand-stitch in place. Topstitch waist-

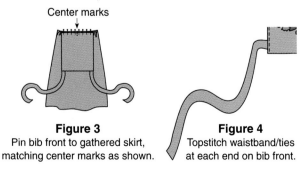

Figure 3
Pin bib front to gathered skirt, matching center marks as shown.

Figure 4
Topstitch waistband/ties at each end on bib front.

band/ties at each end on bib front section to secure as shown in Figure 4.

Step 17. Position pockets 6" down from top edge of skirt and 8" from side of skirt; topstitch in place, leaving top edge open to finish.

Sweatshirt

- **Skill Level:** Beginner
- **Sweatshirt Size:** Adult

- Large tan sweatshirt
- Scrap fabric for appliqué as follows: red/white/green stripe, green dot and red, cream and tan prints
- White all-purpose thread
- All-purpose thread to match fabrics
- 3/8 yard fusible transfer web
- 3/8 yard tear-off fabric stabilizer
- 1 package 7/8" fusible web strip
- 12 (1/2") red buttons
- Red 6-strand embroidery floss
- .05 black permanent fabric pen
- Makeup blusher
- White acrylic paint
- Basic sewing supplies and tools

Instructions

Step 1. Wash all fabrics and sweatshirt; do not use fabric softener.

Step 2. Prepare templates for sweatshirt appliqué and cut referring to Step 5 for apron.

Step 3. Carefully remove ribbing from bottom edge and sleeve cuffs of sweatshirt. Cut a piece of 7/8" fusible transfer strip to fit each cut edge. Fuse to bottom of each cut edge; remove paper backing. Turn to wrong side; fuse in place to make a facing on inside of sweatshirt sleeves and bottom edge.

Step 4. Using 3 strands of red embroidery floss and a large blanket stitch, stitch around bottom and sleeve edges.

Step 5. Arrange one candy cane shape with two

Happy Gingerbread Sweatshirt
Placement Diagram
Adult Size

holly leaves 2" up from bottom edge on center front of sweatshirt; repeat with one motif at each side and one in center back referring to the Placement Diagram and photo of project for positioning. Fuse shapes in place.

Step 6. Repeat with gingerbread boy/girl motif 2 1/2" down from top neck edge on the center front of sweatshirt; fuse shapes in place.

Step 7. Cut a piece of tear-off fabric stabilizer larger than area behind fused shapes; pin to the inside of the sweatshirt behind fused shapes. Using thread to match fabrics, machine-appliqué shapes in place.

Continued on page 115

Holly Leaf
Cut 14 green dot for sweatshirt & 10 green dot for apron

⑧

Gingerbread Boy/Girl
Cut 1 tan print each for apron & sweatshirt

① ④ ③

⑦ ② ⑤

Bow
Cut 1 red print each for apron & sweatshirt

⑥

Apron
Cut 1 cream print for sweatshirt & 1 green print for apron

⑨

Country Christmas Quilting **103**

Reindeer Vest

By Charlyne Stewart

The unique look of this vest is achieved by shadow quilting, layering sheer white fabric over darker colored fabrics.

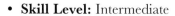

- **Skill Level:** Intermediate
- **Vest Size:** Adult

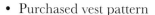

- Purchased vest pattern
- Navy and lining fabrics as specified on vest pattern
- 3/4 yard sheer white fabric
- 3/8 yard quilter's fleece
- 1 yard thin batting
- 1 spool each white and navy all-purpose thread
- 1 spool white quilting thread
- 1 package small pink iridescent snowflake sequins
- 1 package transparent seed beads
- 8 (1/4") pale pink buttons
- Basic sewing supplies and tools

Instructions

Step 1. Prepare templates for each shape using pattern pieces given. Cut as directed on each piece.

Step 2. Cut vest pieces using commercial pattern and instructions. Cut two vest fronts (reverse one) from white sheer fabric and quilter's fleece.

Step 3. Place reindeer and leaf shapes on navy vest fronts referring to the Placement Diagram for positioning. Place white sheer fabric pieces on top of matching front pieces; carefully pin or baste layers together.

Step 4. Using white quilting thread, hand-quilt around reindeer and leaf shapes through all layers. Quilt vertical lines as shown in Figure 1.

Step 5. Finish vest construction as directed in pattern.

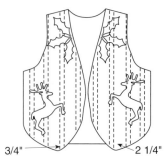

3/4"   2 1/4"

Figure 1
Quilt vertical lines on
fronts as shown.

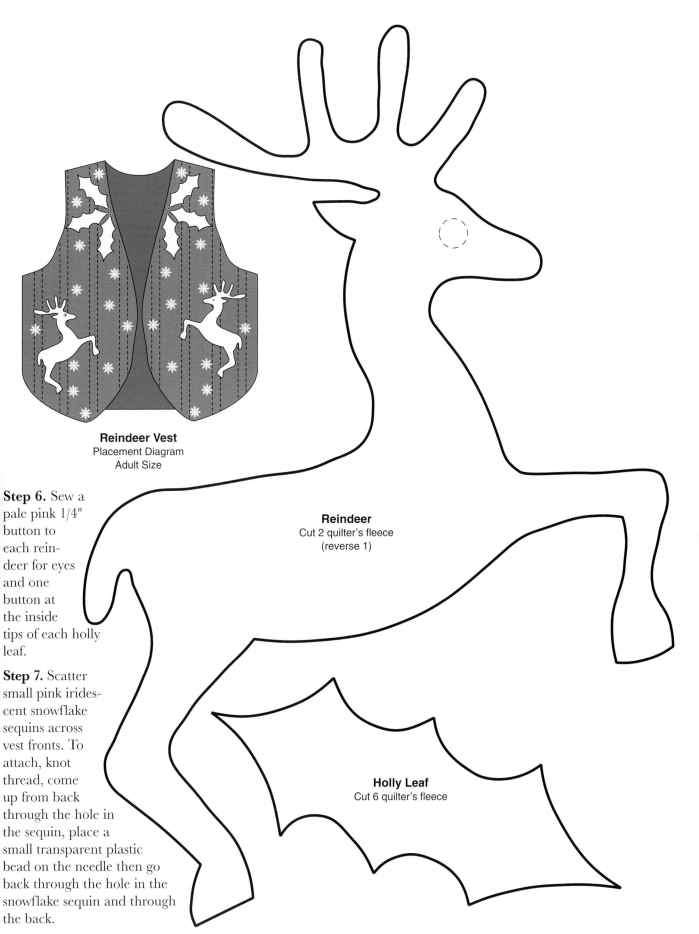

Reindeer Vest
Placement Diagram
Adult Size

Reindeer
Cut 2 quilter's fleece
(reverse 1)

Holly Leaf
Cut 6 quilter's fleece

Step 6. Sew a pale pink 1/4" button to each reindeer for eyes and one button at the inside tips of each holly leaf.

Step 7. Scatter small pink iridescent snowflake sequins across vest fronts. To attach, knot thread, come up from back through the hole in the sequin, place a small transparent plastic bead on the needle then go back through the hole in the snowflake sequin and through the back.

Step 8. Catch the edge of each snowflake sequin; knot off on back to finish. ❀

Mr. & Mrs. Claus

By Joyce Livingston

Santa is mentally reviewing his list to be sure he hasn't forgotten anything while Mrs. Claus is waiting to hand him his mittens and hat. He'll soon be on his way.

- **Skill Level:** Beginner
- **Cardigan Size:** Adult

- Large blue sweatshirt
- Scrap fabric for appliqué as follows: red, white, green, gray and gold prints, and black and tan solids
- All-purpose thread to match fabrics
- 1 yard fusible transfer web
- 3/8 yard tear-off fabric stabilizer
- Red yarn
- 12 assorted red and green buttons
- .05 black and red permanent fabric pens
- White acrylic paint
- Makeup blusher
- Fade-out pen
- Basic sewing supplies and tools, toothpick and carpet needle

Instructions

Step 1. Wash all fabrics and sweatshirt; do not use fabric softener.

Step 2. Prepare templates for each appliqué shape using pattern pieces given. Trace shapes onto paper side of fusible transfer web. Cut out each shape leaving a margin around traced lines.

Step 3. Fuse shapes to fabric scraps referring to patterns for color suggestions and number to cut. Cut shapes on traced lines; remove paper backing.

Step 4. Mark center front line on sweatshirt using fade-out pen. Cut along center front line; carefully remove all ribbing from sweatshirt bottom, cuffs and neck edge.

Step 5. Cut a piece of 7/8" fusible transfer web to fit each cut edge. Fuse to bottom of each cut edge; remove paper backing. Turn to wrong side; fuse in place to make a facing on inside of sweatshirt sleeves, neckline, front opening and bottom edge.

Step 6. Thread carpet needle with red yarn; slipstitch around all outer edges of sweatshirt.

Step 7. Arrange Mrs. Claus and Santa motifs and trees with stars on the sweatshirt front referring to the Placement Diagram and photo of project for

paint with toothpick to eyes for highlight. Use make-up blusher to add cheek color.

Step 9. Stitch assorted red and green buttons to trees and stars referring to the Placement Diagram and project photo for positioning. ❦

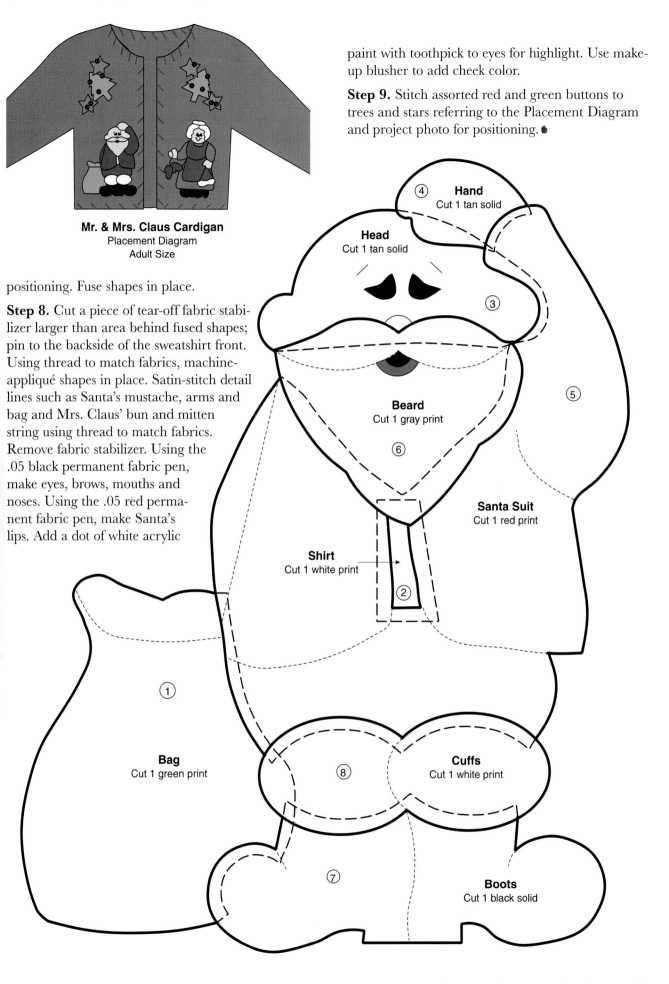

Mr. & Mrs. Claus Cardigan
Placement Diagram
Adult Size

positioning. Fuse shapes in place.

Step 8. Cut a piece of tear-off fabric stabilizer larger than area behind fused shapes; pin to the backside of the sweatshirt front. Using thread to match fabrics, machine-appliqué shapes in place. Satin-stitch detail lines such as Santa's mustache, arms and bag and Mrs. Claus' bun and mitten string using thread to match fabrics. Remove fabric stabilizer. Using the .05 black permanent fabric pen, make eyes, brows, mouths and noses. Using the .05 red permanent fabric pen, make Santa's lips. Add a dot of white acrylic

④ **Hand**
Cut 1 tan solid

Head
Cut 1 tan solid

③

⑤

Beard
Cut 1 gray print

⑥

Santa Suit
Cut 1 red print

Shirt
Cut 1 white print

②

Bag
Cut 1 green print

①

Cuffs
Cut 1 white print

⑧

Boots
Cut 1 black solid

⑦

Tree
Cut 2 green print

Hair
Cut 1 white print

Face
Cut 1 tan solid

⑨

⑧

Hand
Cut 1 tan solid

②

Hand
Cut 1 tan solid

⑦

④

Mittens
Cut 1 red print

⑩

Apron
Cut 1 red print

⑤

Hat
Cut 1 red print

Dress
Cut 1 green print

③

Brim
Cut 1 white print

⑥

Star
Cut 4 gold print

Shoes
Cut 1 black solid

①

Tied Up for Christmas

By Karen Neary

Stitch a fun holiday tie for the special man in your life using simple patchwork and appliqué designs.

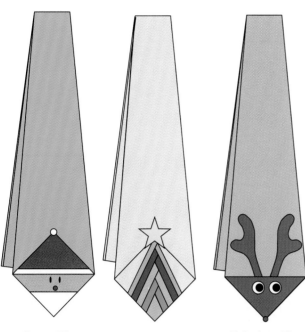

Santa Tie
Placement Diagram

Christmas Tree Tie
Placement Diagram

Reindeer Tie
Placement Diagram

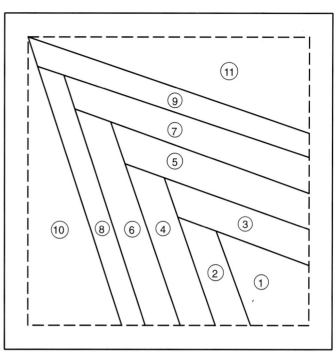

Foundation for Christmas Tree Block
Use green scraps for pieces 1–9; use cream
print for pieces 10 and 11.

Project Notes

Purchase a commercial tie pattern.
Use the tie tip pattern given to adjust
commercial pattern to fit patchwork.
Prepare patchwork or appliqué sections before constructing tie as
instructed on commercial pattern.

Christmas Tree
3" x 3" Block

Christmas Tree Tie

- **Skill Level:** Intermediate
- **Block Size:** 3" x 3"

- Commercial pattern for adult-size tie
- Cream print fabric for tie and lining and
  notions as listed on pattern
- Scraps of 5 different green prints
- All-purpose thread to match fabrics
- 1/8 yard tear-off fabric stabilizer
- 1 1/2" gold star button
- Basic sewing supplies and tools and
  fade-out pen

Instructions

Step 1. Cut pieces for tie using commercial pattern
combined with tie-tip pattern given.

Step 2. Using fade-out pen, draw a line 3 1/4" up
from and parallel to the left side of point as shown in
Figure 1.

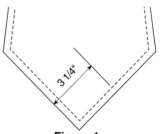

3 1/4"

Figure 1
Mark tip of tie as shown.

Step 3. Trace pattern for tree block onto tear-off fabric stabilizer. Cut fabric scraps larger than shapes on
pattern. Pin piece 1 onto unmarked side of marked
stabilizer base. Place piece 2 right sides together with
piece 1; on marked side of stabilizer, stitch on line
between pieces 1 and 2.

Step 4. Press piece 2 open; trim 1/4" from seam lines,
if necessary. Place piece 3 right sides together with
piece 2. Stitch as in Step 3; press piece 3 open.
Continue adding pieces in numerical order until all
pieces have been added.

Step 5. Trim stitched square to size of stabilizer base;
carefully remove stabilizer.

Step 6. With right side of stitched tree block facing up, fold under seam allowance on the top left side as shown in Figure 2; press. Fold under seam allowance on top right side; press to marked seam line.

Figure 2
Press seam allowance under on top left side.

Step 7. Lay block right side up in position on tie; flip block back along the right seam allowance so that the right side of the block is facing the right side of the tie. Pressed seam line on block should be aligned with line drawn on tie front in Step 2. Stitch across this seam.

Step 8. Fold block back down; press. Hand-stitch pressed left side of block to tie.

Step 9. Finish tie as instructed with commercial tie pattern.

Step 10. Sew 1 1/2" gold star button to top of tree to finish.

Santa
3" x 3" Block

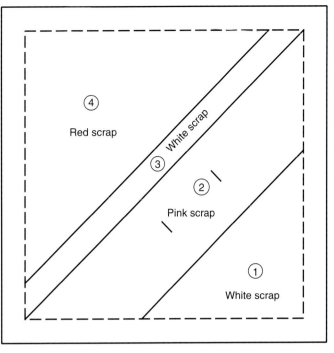

Foundation for Santa Block

Santa Tie

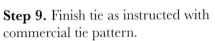

- **Skill Level:** Intermediate
- **Block Size:** 3" x 3"

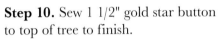

- Commercial pattern for adult-size tie
- Fabrics for tie and lining and notions as listed on pattern
- Scraps of white, red and pink
- All-purpose thread to match fabrics
- Black all-purpose thread
- 1/8 yard tear-off fabric stabilizer
- 1/4" red pompom
- 3/8" white pompom
- Basic sewing supplies and tools and fade-out pen

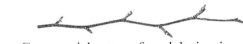

Instructions

Step 1. Prepare tie as in Steps 1 and 2 for Christmas Tree Tie.

Step 2. Trace pattern for Santa block onto tear-off fabric stabilizer.

Step 3. Piece Santa block and finish tie referring to Steps 3–9 for Christmas Tree Tie.

Step 4. Hand-stitch 3/8" white pompon to top of pieced Santa and 1/4" red pompom to pink area for nose. Hand-stitch two lines as marked on pattern using black all-purpose thread to make eyes.

Reindeer Tie

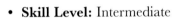

- **Skill Level:** Intermediate
- **Design Area:** Approximately 4 1/4" x 4 3/4" at tie tip

- Commercial pattern for adult-size tie
- Fabrics for tie and lining and notions as listed on pattern
- 2 squares brown print 3 1/2" x 3 1/2"
- All-purpose thread to match fabrics
- 1 spool gold machine-embroidery thread
- 3 1/2" x 3 1/2" square fusible transfer web
- 2 (1/2") sew-on wiggle eyes
- 1/4" red bead
- Basic sewing supplies and tools

Instructions

Step 1. Prepare tie as in Step 1 for Christmas Tree Tie.

Step 2. Fold one 3 1/2" x 3 1/2" brown print square in half on one diagonal wrong sides together; press.

Step 3. Pin in place on tie point with raw edges even as shown in Figure 3.

Step 4. Fuse the 3 1/2" x 3 1/2" square fusible transfer web to the wrong side of the remaining 3 1/2" x 3 1/2" brown print square.

Step 5. Prepare pattern for antler shape. Trace two antlers onto paper side of fused square, reversing one antler. Cut out on traced lines; remove paper backing.

Step 6. Position antlers on tie, slipping bottom of antlers underneath the top fold of the pinned triangle; remove triangle.

Step 7. Machine-appliqué antlers in place using gold machine-embroidery thread and a narrow zigzag stitch.

Step 8. Lay folded triangle back in place with raw edges even; pin bottom layer in place. Unfold triangle; using matching all-

purpose thread, stitch along fold line through all layers.

Step 9. Flip triangle back in place; baste raw edges in place.

Step 10. Finish tie as instructed with commercial tie pattern.

Step 11. Hand-stitch 1/2" wiggle eyes and 1/4" red-bead nose in place to finish. ●

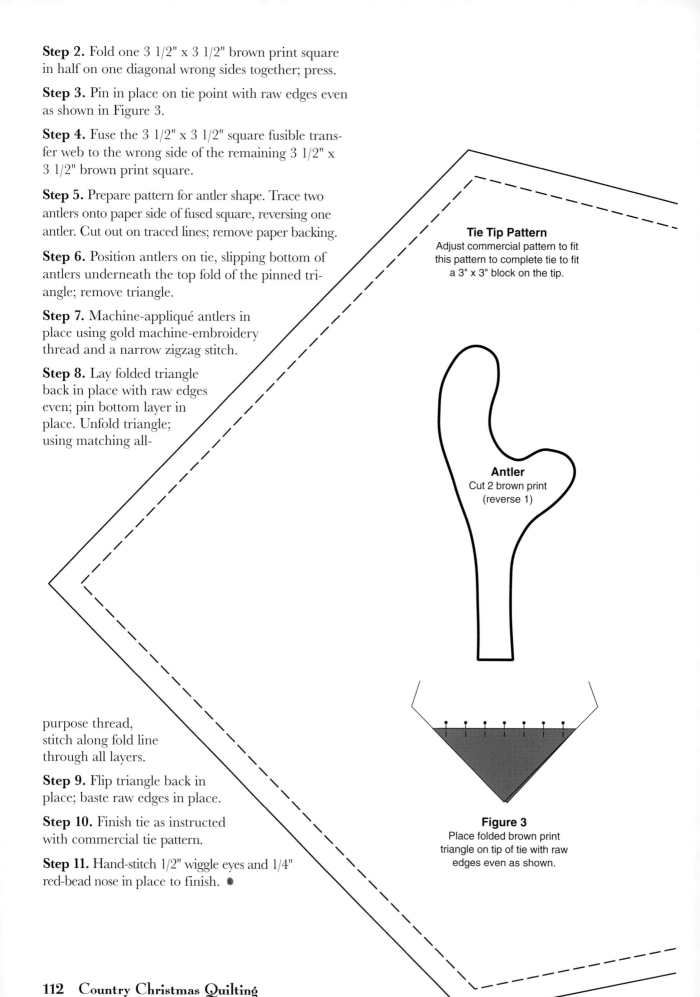

Tie Tip Pattern
Adjust commercial pattern to fit this pattern to complete tie to fit a 3" x 3" block on the tip.

Antler
Cut 2 brown print
(reverse 1)

Figure 3
Place folded brown print triangle on tip of tie with raw edges even as shown.

Santa Jingles Sweatshirt

By Beth Wheeler

anta only comes once a year, so let your child get dressed up for the occasion. She'll enjoy the jingle of the bells used to trim Santa's hat.

- **Skill Level:** Intermediate
- **Sweatshirt Size:** Child

- 6" x 6" square each red pin dot and peach solid
- 6" x 12" rectangle white solid
- 7" x 14" rectangle white synthetic fur
- White sweatshirt with set-in sleeves
- All-purpose thread to match fabrics
- 3 1/2 yards 1/4"-wide red satin ribbon
- 4 (1/8") black ball buttons
- 2 (3/8") pearl ball buttons
- 2 (1 1/8") jingle bells
- 2 (1 1/2") safety pins
- Fabric glue
- Basic sewing supplies and tools

Project Notes

An adult size small sweatshirt was used for fuller sleeves and trunk. Choose a good-quality, 100 percent cotton or polyester blend sweatshirt. Prewash and dry the sweatshirt; do not use fabric softener. Press to remove wrinkles. The sleeves were cut to a length to fit a child.

A 1/4" seam allowance is used throughout; please read all instructions before beginning project.

Instructions

Step 1. Prepare templates for each shape using pat-

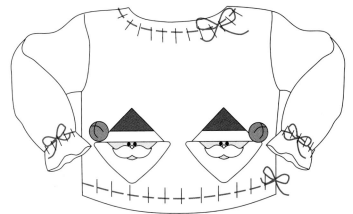

Santa Jingles Sweatshirt
Placement Diagram
Child Size

tern pieces given. Cut as directed on each piece.

Step 2. Place one red pin-dot and one peach solid triangle right sides together; stitch along long edge. Press seams toward red pin dot; repeat.

Step 3. Using the square stitched in Step 2 as a pattern, cut two white solid squares.

Step 4. Place a white solid square right sides together with a stitched square; stitch all around, leaving a 2" opening in the peach solid half as shown in Figure 1. Trim corners; turn right side out. Hand-stitch opening closed.

Figure 1
Stitch layers together leaving an opening in the peach solid side.

Step 5. Cut ribbing from hem of sweatshirt. Trim edge even. Position pieced and lined squares on sweatshirt front referring to photo of project and

Figure 2
Stitch around 3 sides
to make pockets.

Figure 3
Cut slits 1" from hemmed edge
and 1" apart as shown.

Placement Diagram for positioning. Stitch around three sides to make pockets as shown in Figure 2.

Step 6. Position beards on faces; hand-stitch or glue in place. Repeat with mustache and hat trim pieces.

Step 7. Stitch two black ball buttons and one pearl button just above mustache; pin jingle bells in place from inside sweatshirt.

Step 8. Turn neck ribbing to wrong side; pin and stitch close to seam. Trim ribbing off close to seam.

Step 9. Cut sleeves to desired length; stitch a narrow hem around sleeves and bottom of sweatshirt.

Step 10. Cut slits 1" away from sleeve, neckline and bottom edges of sweatshirt as shown in Figure 3. Cut two pieces 1/4"-wide red satin ribbon 18" long, one piece 38" long and one piece 50" long. Weave the shorter pieces in and out of sleeve slits. Gather sleeve on ribbon until it fits a child's wrist; tie ribbon in a bow. Repeat with bottom edge using 50" length and neck edge using 38" length, tying bows in front. ●

Beard
Cut 2 white synthetic fur

Mustache
Cut 2 white synthetic fur

A
Cut 2 each red pin
dot & peach solid

Hat Trim
Cut 2 white
synthetic fur

Happy Gingerbread

continued from page 103

Using white all-purpose thread, make a decorative scallop stitch on each gingerbread boy/girl arm. Remove fabric stabilizer. Using the .05 black permanent fabric pen, make eyes, mouths and noses. Add a dot of white acrylic paint to eyes for highlight. Use makeup blusher to add cheek color.

Step 8. Stitch two 1/2" red buttons to each candy cane motif and four 1/2" red buttons to gingerbread boy/girl motif referring to the Placement Diagram and project photo for positioning.

Holly Leaf
Cut 14 green dot for sweatshirt &
10 green dot for apron

Candy Cane
Cut 2 red/white/green stripe for sweatshirt &
4 red/wite/grees stripe for apron

Santa's on His Way

By Janice Loewenthal

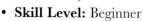

Santa's train is speeding down the tracks trying to get to your house in time for Christmas.

- **Skill Level:** Beginner
- **Sweatshirt Size:** Child

- Child's blue sweatshirt
- Scrap fabric for appliqué as follows: red, blue, white, gray and gold prints, and black and tan solids
- All-purpose thread to match fabrics
- 1/4 yard fusible transfer web
- 1/4 yard tear-off fabric stabilizer
- 1 (5/8") white button
- 1 (5/8") gold button
- 2 (1/2") gold buttons
- .05 black and red permanent fabric pens
- White acrylic paint
- Makeup blusher
- Basic sewing supplies and tools and toothpick

Instructions

Step 1. Wash all fabrics and sweatshirt; do not use fabric softener.

Step 2. Prepare templates for each appliqué shape using pattern pieces given. Trace shapes onto paper side of fusible transfer web. Cut out each shape leaving a margin around traced lines.

Step 3. Fuse shapes to fabric scraps referring to patterns for color suggestions and number to cut.

Cut shapes on traced lines; remove paper backing.

Step 4. Arrange appliqué motifs and stars on the sweatshirt center front referring to the Placement Diagram and photo of project for positioning. Fuse shapes in place.

Step 5. Cut a piece of tear-off fabric stabilizer larger than area behind fused shapes; pin to the backside of the sweatshirt. Using thread to match fabrics, machine-appliqué shapes in place. Remove fabric stabilizer. Using the .05 black permanent fabric pen, make eyes and mouth; using the .05 red permanet fabric pen, make lip. Add a dot of white acrylic paint

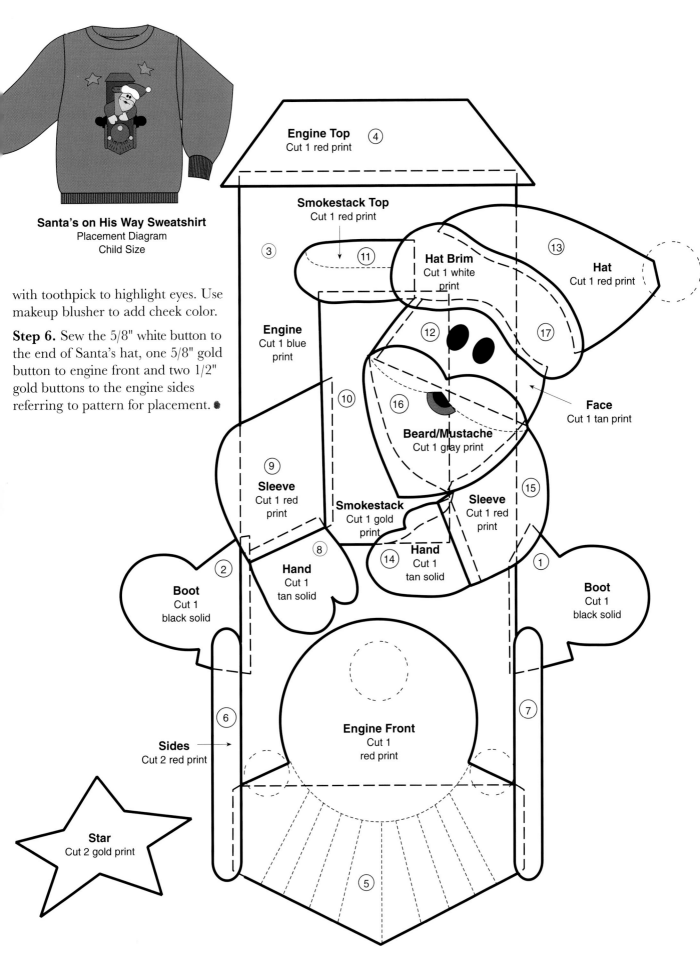

Santa's on His Way Sweatshirt
Placement Diagram
Child Size

with toothpick to highlight eyes. Use makeup blusher to add cheek color.

Step 6. Sew the 5/8" white button to the end of Santa's hat, one 5/8" gold button to engine front and two 1/2" gold buttons to the engine sides referring to pattern for placement. ●

Engine Top ④
Cut 1 red print

③

Smokestack Top
Cut 1 red print

⑪

Engine
Cut 1 blue
print

Hat Brim
Cut 1 white
print

⑬ **Hat**
Cut 1 red print

⑫

⑰

Face
Cut 1 tan print

⑩

⑯

Beard/Mustache
Cut 1 gray print

Sleeve
Cut 1 red
print
⑨

Smokestack
Cut 1 gold
print

Sleeve
Cut 1 red
print
⑮

Boot
Cut 1
black solid
②

⑧

Hand
Cut 1
tan solid

Hand
Cut 1
tan solid
⑭

①

Boot
Cut 1
black solid

⑥

Sides →
Cut 2 red print

Engine Front
Cut 1
red print

⑦

Star
Cut 2 gold print

⑤

Make a Joyful Noise

By Janice Loewenthal

 purchased felt vest may be embellished with a holiday motif for a quick fashion statement. It's quick, easy and ready to wear tonight.

Make a Joyful Noise
Placement Diagram
Adult Size

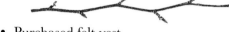

- **Skill Level:** Beginner
- **Vest Size:** Adult

- Purchased felt vest
- 7" x 7" square matching felt for pocket
- Scraps for appliqué in the following colors: green dot, cream, tan, brown, white, burgundy and gold
- All-purpose thread to match appliqué fabrics
- 1/2 yard fusible transfer web
- 1/3 yard tear-off fabric stabilizer
- Fade-out pen
- .05 black permanent fabric pen
- White acrylic paint
- Assorted burgundy and green buttons
- Black 6-strand embroidery floss
- Makeup blusher
- Basic sewing supplies and tools and toothpick

Instructions

Step 1. Wash all scraps; do not use fabric softener.

Step 2. Prepare templates for each shape using pattern pieces given. Trace shapes onto paper side of fusible transfer web. Cut out each shape leaving a margin around traced lines.

Step 3. Fuse shapes to fabric scraps referring to patterns for color suggestions. Cut shapes on traced lines; remove paper backing.

Step 4. Cut out pocket from matching felt square. Center wreath and banner shapes on pocket, layering as necessary; fuse in place.

Step 5. Cut a piece of tear-off fabric stabilizer larger than fused shapes; pin to the backside of the pocket. Using thread to match fabrics, machine-appliqué shapes in place. Remove fabric stabilizer. Using the .05 black permanent fabric pen, write message on banner.

Step 6. Pin pocket to vest left front as shown in Figure 1. Using 3 strands black embroidery floss, blanket-stitch pocket to vest and across pocket top.

Step 7. Repeat appliqué process for design for vest

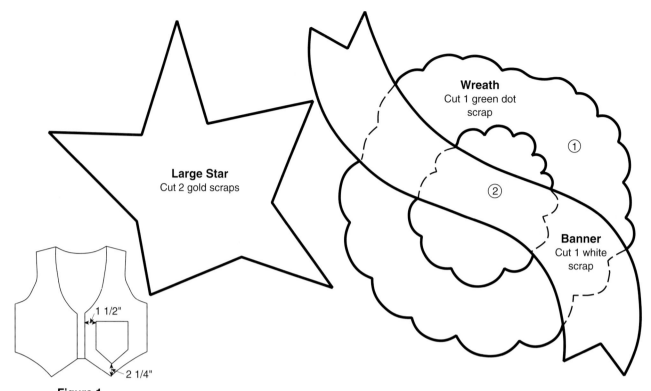

Large Star
Cut 2 gold scraps

Wreath
Cut 1 green dot
scrap

① ②

Banner
Cut 1 white
scrap

1 1/2"

2 1/4"

Figure 1
Pin pocket to left
vest front as
shown.

Pocket
Cut 1 felt

right front and stars referring to the Placement Diagram and photo for positioning.

Step 8. Hand-stitch buttons in place on stars, wreath design and tree design as desired and referring to the photo of the project for positioning suggestions. Satin-stitch detail lines such as bird's beak, wing and lines on bunny using threads to match fabrics or colors as desired.

Step 9. Draw eyes on bird, moose and bunny, nose and mouth on moose and bunny using .05 black permanent fabric pen. Add a dot of white acrylic paint with toothpick to highlight eyes. Use makeup blusher to add cheek color.

Step 10. Using 3 strands black embroidery floss, blanket-stitch around all outside edges of vest to finish. ●

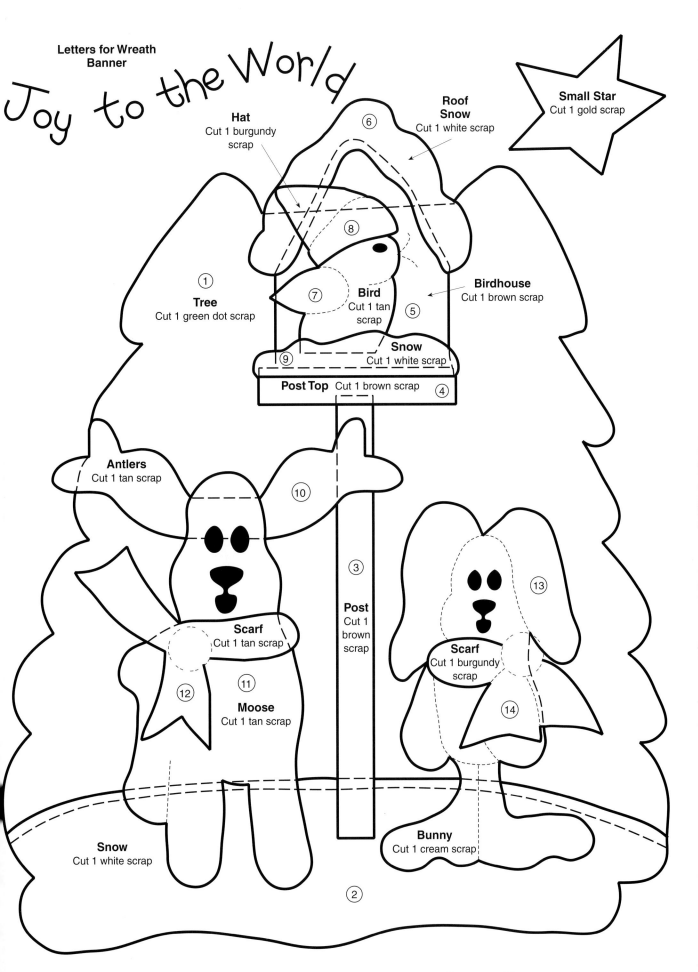

Letters for Wreath Banner

Joy to the World

Hat Cut 1 burgundy scrap

Roof Snow Cut 1 white scrap

Small Star Cut 1 gold scrap

⑥

⑧

Bird Cut 1 tan scrap

Birdhouse Cut 1 brown scrap

①

Tree Cut 1 green dot scrap

⑦

⑤

Snow Cut 1 white scrap

⑨

Post Top Cut 1 brown scrap ④

Antlers Cut 1 tan scrap

⑩

③

Post Cut 1 brown scrap

Scarf Cut 1 tan scrap

Scarf Cut 1 burgundy scrap

⑬

⑫

⑪

Moose Cut 1 tan scrap

⑭

Snow Cut 1 white scrap

Bunny Cut 1 cream scrap

②

Homespun Holiday Quilts

Stitch a collection of country Christmas quilts that will go with any decor from a primitive rustic look to a traditional classic style. While most are in the traditional red and green Christmas colors, you'll also find a few surprises, like our Blue Christmas quilt. Other quilts feature stars, trees, poinsettias, and even outdoor scenes. Share the meaning of Christmas with all your family and friends with the gift of a Christmas quilt.

Holiday Village

By Jill Reber

Pieced house, star and tree blocks combine with country colors and homespun fabrics to make this pretty holiday wall quilt. It also makes a great house warming gift.

- **Skill Level:** Beginner
- **Quilt Size:** 32" x 40"
- **Block Sizes:** 4" x 4", 4" x 8" and 8" x 8"
- **Number of Blocks:** 4 Four-Patch, 1 Star, 4 Tree and 4 House blocks

- 1/8 yard gold print
- 1/3 yard red print
- 1/4 yard each blue and green prints
- 2/3 yard burgundy print
- 3/4 yard off-white print
- 1 1/2" x 12" piece brown check
- Batting 36" x 44"
- Backing 36" x 44"
- 4 1/2 yards self-made or purchased binding
- Coordinating all-purpose thread
- Off-white linen thread
- 4 gold wooden star buttons
- Basic sewing supplies and tools

House Blocks

Step 1. Cut one strip off-white print 4 7/8" by fabric width; subcut into 4 7/8" segments. You will need four segments. Cut each segment in half on one diagonal to make eight A triangles.

Step 2. Cut one square red print 9 1/4" x 9 1/4". Cut square on both diagonals to make four B triangles.

Step 3. Cut one strip blue print 3 1/2" by fabric width; cut strip into 22" segments. Cut one strip gold print 2 1/2" x 22". Sew the gold print strip between two blue print strips along length. Press seams toward blue print strips. Cut into four 3 1/2" segments for C-D units.

Step 4. Cut one strip blue print 1 1/2" by fabric width; subcut into four 8 1/2" strips for E.

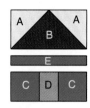 

Figure 1
Sew A to each side of B; join with C-D and E to complete 1 House block.

Figure 2
Join 3 E-F units with a G-H unit to complete 1 Tree block.

Step 5. Sew an A triangle to each angled side of B. Join with C-D and E to complete one house block as shown in Figure 1; repeat for four blocks. Press seams in one direction; set aside.

Tree Blocks

Step 1. Cut one strip off-white print 2 7/8" by fabric width. Subcut into twelve 2 7/8" squares. Cut each square on one diagonal to make 24 E triangles.

Step 2. Cut three squares green print 5 1/4" x 5 1/4"; cut each square on both diagonals to make 12 F triangles.

Step 3. Cut two strips off-white print 2" x 12". Sew the 1 1/2" x 12" brown check strip between the two off-white print strips along length; press seams toward brown check strip. Subcut into four 2 1/2" segments for G-H units.

Step 4. Sew an E triangle to each angled side of F; repeat for 12 E-F units.

Step 5. Join three E-F units with a G-H unit as shown in

Holiday Village
Placement Diagram
32" x 40"

Four-Patch
4" x 4" Block
Make 4

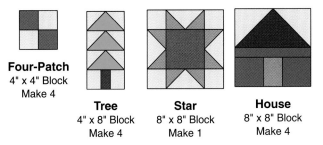

Tree
4" x 8" Block
Make 4

Star
8" x 8" Block
Make 1

House
8" x 8" Block
Make 4

Figure 2 to complete one block; repeat for four blocks.

Star Block

Step 1. Cut one square off-white print 5 1/4" x 5 1/4"; cut on both diagonals to make four I triangles.

Step 2. Cut four squares off-white print 2 1/2" x 2 1/2" for J.

Step 3. Cut four squares gold print 2 7/8" x 2 7/8". Cut each square in half on one diagonal to make eight K triangles.

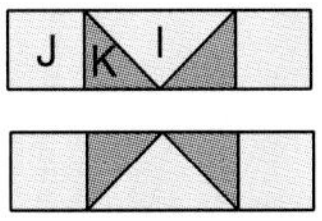

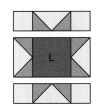

Figure 3
Sew J to each end
of 2 K-I units.

Figure 4
Join pieced units as
shown to complete
1 Star block.

Step 4. Cut one square burgundy print 4 1/2" x 4 1/2" for L.

Step 5. Sew two K triangles to I; repeat for four units. Sew a J square to each end of two units as shown in Figure 3. Sew a K-I unit to two opposite sides of L. Join the pieced units as shown in Figure 4 to complete one block.

Quilt Assembly

Step 1. Join two House blocks with one Tree block to make a row as shown in Figure 5; repeat for two rows. Press seams in one direction.

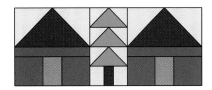

Figure 5
Join blocks to make a row as shown.

Step 2. Cut four strips off-white print 1 1/2" x 8 1/2". Join two Tree blocks with the Star block and off-white print strips to make a row as shown in Figure 6; press seams in one direction.

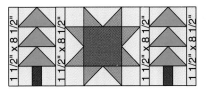

Figure 6
Join blocks and strips to make a row as shown.

Step 3. Cut four strips off-white print 2 1/2" x 20 1/2". Join the block rows with these strips as shown in Figure 7; press seams toward strips.

Continued on page 154

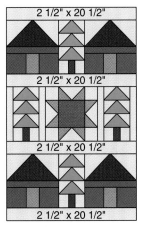

Figure 7
Join block rows with 2 1/2" x 20 1/2"
off-white print strips.

Christmas Star

By Jill Reber

Make this star design in Christmas colors for a pretty accent and use as a table cover or wall quilt to add to your holiday decor.

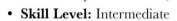

- **Skill Level:** Intermediate
- **Quilt Size:** 44" x 44"
- **Block Size:** 8" x 8" and 24" x 24"
- **Number of Blocks:** 4 small and 1 large

- 1/2 yard green print
- 3/8 yard red print
- 2 yards tan mottled
- Batting 48" x 48"
- Backing 48" x 48"
- 5 1/2 yards self-made or purchased binding
- All-purpose thread to match fabrics
- Basic sewing supplies and tools

Center Star Block

Step 1. Cut the following from tan mottled: two squares 9 1/4" x 9 1/4" for A; two squares 5 1/4" x 5 1/4" for B; one 8 1/2" x 8 1/2" square for C; and one strip 4 1/2" by fabric width and subcut into eight 4 1/2" squares for D.

Step 2. Cut the following from red print: one 9 1/4" x 9 1/4" square for A; and four 3 3/8" x 3 3/8" squares for E.

Step 3. Cut one strip green print 4 7/8" by fabric width for F. Cut strip into 4 7/8" square units; you will need eight squares. Cut each square on one diagonal to make F triangles; you will need 16 F triangles.

Step 4. Cut the 9 1/4" x 9 1/4" red print and tan mottled A squares in half on both diagonals to make four A triangles from each square; you will need eight tan mottled and four red print A triangles.

Step 5. Cut the 5 1/4" x 5 1/4" tan mottled B squares in half on both diagonals to make B triangles. You will need eight B triangles.

Step 6. Sew a B triangle to two adjacent sides of E as shown in Figure 1; add F to each end. Repeat for four units.

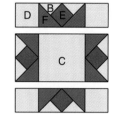

Figure 1
Sew B to adjacent
sides of E; add F.

Figure 2
Join units to complete
center unit.

Step 7. Sew a D to each end of two units. Sew the remaining two units to opposite sides of C. Join the pieced units as shown in Figure 2 to complete the center unit.

Step 8. Sew two tan mottled A's to one red print A; sew F to each end referring to Figure 3; repeat for four units. Sew a unit to two opposite sides of the pieced center unit. Sew a D square to each end of the remaining two units; sew to remaining sides of pieced unit referring to Figure 4 to complete Center Star block.

Corner Star Blocks

Step 1. Cut one strip tan mottled 2 1/2" by fabric width; subcut into 2 1/2" square segments for G squares. You will need 16 G squares.

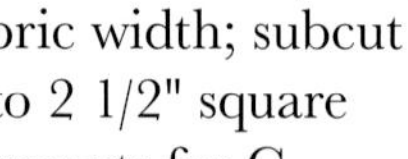

Figure 3
Sew F to each end
of the A unit.

Figure 4
Join units to complete
center block as shown.

Christmas Star
Placement Diagram
44" x 44"

Center Star
24" x 24" Block

Corner Star
8" x 8" Block

Step 2. Cut four squares tan mottled 5 1/4" x 5 1/4". Cut each square in half on both diagonals to make H triangles; you will need 16 H triangles.

Step 3. Cut 16 squares red print 2 7/8" x 2 7/8". Cut each square in half on one diagonal to make J triangles; you will need 32 J triangles.

Step 4. Cut four squares red print 4 1/2" x 4 1/2" for I.

Step 5. To complete one corner block, sew J to two adjacent sides of H as shown in Figure 5; repeat for four units.

Figure 5
Sew J to H as shown.

Step 6. Sew a pieced unit to opposite sides of I. Sew G to each end of the remaining two units; sew these units to the previously pieced unit as shown in Figure 6 to complete one Corner Star block. Repeat for four blocks.

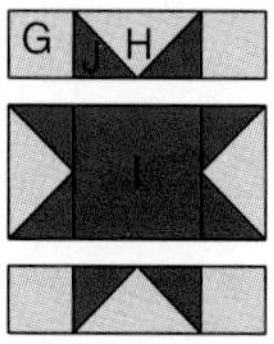

Figure 6
Join units to complete
1 corner block.

Flying Geese

Step 1. Cut four strips tan mottled 2 7/8" by fabric width. Cut into 2 7/8" square segments for J; you will need 48 squares. Cut each square in half on one diagonal to make J triangles; you will need 96 J triangles.

Step 2. Cut two strips green print 5 1/4" by fabric width. Cut in 12 square segments for K. Cut each square in half on both diagonals to make K triangles; you will need 48 K triangles.

Step 3. Sew J to two adjacent sides of K to make one Flying Geese unit as shown in Figure 7; repeat for 48 units.

Figure 7
Sew J to K to make 1
Flying Geese unit.

Step 4. Join 12 Flying Geese units to make a strip as shown in Figure 8; repeat for four strips.

Figure 8
Join 12 Flying Geese units as shown.

Step 5. Cut four strips tan mottled 4 1/2" x 24 1/2". Sew a strip to one side of each Flying Geese strip as shown in Figure 9; press seams toward tan mottled strips.

4 1/2" x 24 1/2"

Figure 9
Sew a 4 1/2" x 24 1/2" strip to 1
side of the Flying Geese strip.

Top Construction

Step 1. Sew a Flying Geese strip to opposite sides of the pieced center block; press seams toward strips.

Step 2. Sew a Corner Star block to each end of the remaining two Flying Geese strips; press seams toward strips. Sew a strip to the two remaining sides of the pieced center; press seams toward strips.

Step 3. Cut two strips each tan mottled 2 1/2" x 40 1/2" and 2 1/2" x 44 1/2". Sew shorter strips to two opposite sides and longer strips to remaining sides; press seams toward strips to complete pieced top.

Step 4. Prepare for quilting and finish referring to General Instructions. ●

Poinsettias

By Jill Reber

Poinsettia plants add color to any Christmas decor. Make this pretty wall quilt in similar colors to add to the theme. You'll enjoy making the flowers with these easy-to-follow instructions.

- **Skill Level:** Intermediate
- **Quilt Size:** 57 1/4" x 57 1/4"
- **Block Size:** 16" x 16"
- **Number of Blocks:** 4

- 2/3 yard dark green solid
- 1/4 yard medium red print
- 5/8 yard light red print
- 1/2 yard each dark red and dark green prints
- 1 yard muslin
- 1 1/2 yards red-and-green print
- Batting 62" x 62"
- Backing 62" x 62"
- 7 yards self-made or purchased binding
- All-purpose thread to match fabrics
- Basic sewing supplies and tools

Instructions

Step 1. Prepare templates using pattern pieces given; cut as directed on each piece.

Step 2. To make one Flower Unit A, sew a dark green print C to a muslin F to a dark red print C; repeat in opposite color order as shown in Figure 1.

Step 3. Sew a dark red print C to each short side of a muslin F as shown in Figure 2; repeat.

Make 1   Make 1

Figure 1
Sew C to F to C.

Figure 2
Sew C to F to C.

Step 4. Sew a dark red print D to a dark green print D; sew to B as shown in Figure 3.

The Poinsettias Placement Diagram and block images:

Poinsettias
Placement Diagram
57 1/4" x 57 1/4"

Poinsettia
16" x 16" Block

Figure 3
Sew D to D; sew to B.

Figure 4
Arrange pieced units with D to make Flower Unit A.

Step 5. Arrange pieced units with muslin D pieces as shown in Figure 4. Join in rows; join rows to complete one Flower Unit A.

Step 6. To make one Flower Unit B, sew a dark green print C to each short side of a muslin F; sew a dark red print C to each short side of a muslin F; and sew a dark red print C to each short side of a dark green print F referring to Figure 5. Sew the last C-F unit to a dark red print B.

Figure 5
Sew C pieces to F as shown.

Step 7. Arrange pieced units with muslin D pieces as shown in Figure 6. Join in rows; join rows to complete one Flower Unit B. Repeat for two units.

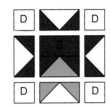

Figure 6
Arrange pieced units with D
to make Flower Unit B.

Step 8. To make a Basket Unit, sew a muslin A to a medium red print A. Sew a medium red print C to one end of a muslin B; turn C and sew to muslin B as shown in Figure 7. Sew the C-B units to the A units; add E to complete Basket Unit as shown in Figure 8.

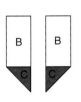

Figure 7
Sew C to B as shown.

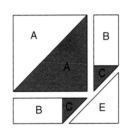

Figure 8
Join units to complete
1 Basket Unit.

Step 9. Join one Flower Unit A with two Flower Unit B's and one Basket Unit to complete one block as shown in Figure 9; repeat for four blocks and press.

Figure 9
Join 1 Flower Unit A with 2
Flower Unit B's and 1 Basket
Unit to complete 1 block.

Step 10. To make stems, cut two strips 1 1/2" by fabric width green solid. Fold the strips in half along length with wrong sides together; press. Fold strips just shy of in half again; press.

Step 11. Place strips for flower stems as shown in Figure 10, trimming 1/2" longer than needed for each piece. Fold under ends; pin in place. Machine-stitch down the center of each strip; hand-appliqué edges of strips down.

Figure 10
Place strips on block as shown.

Figure 11
Join blocks to complete
center as shown.

Step 12. Join the four blocks referring to Figure 11 to complete pieced center.

Step 13. Cut eight strips green solid 2 1/2" x 25". Cut two squares light red print 19 1/2" x 19 1/2". Cut each square in half on one diagonal to make triangles; you will need four triangles.

Step 14. Sew a 2 1/2" x 25" strip green solid to one

Figure 12
Trim strip even with
edge of triangle.

Figure 13
Trim strip as shown.

short side of one triangle; press and trim even with edge of triangle as shown in Figure 12. Sew another 2 1/2" x 25" strip green solid to the remaining short side of the triangle as shown in Figure 13; press and trim as before. Repeat for all four triangles.

Step 15. Sew a bordered triangle to each side of the pieced center; press seams toward triangles.

Step 16. Cut and piece four strips red-and-green print 6 1/2" x 60". Center strips on pieced center; stitch to sides, mitering corners. Trim excess at corner miters; press seams open.

Step 17. Prepare for quilting and finish referring to General Instructions. ❧

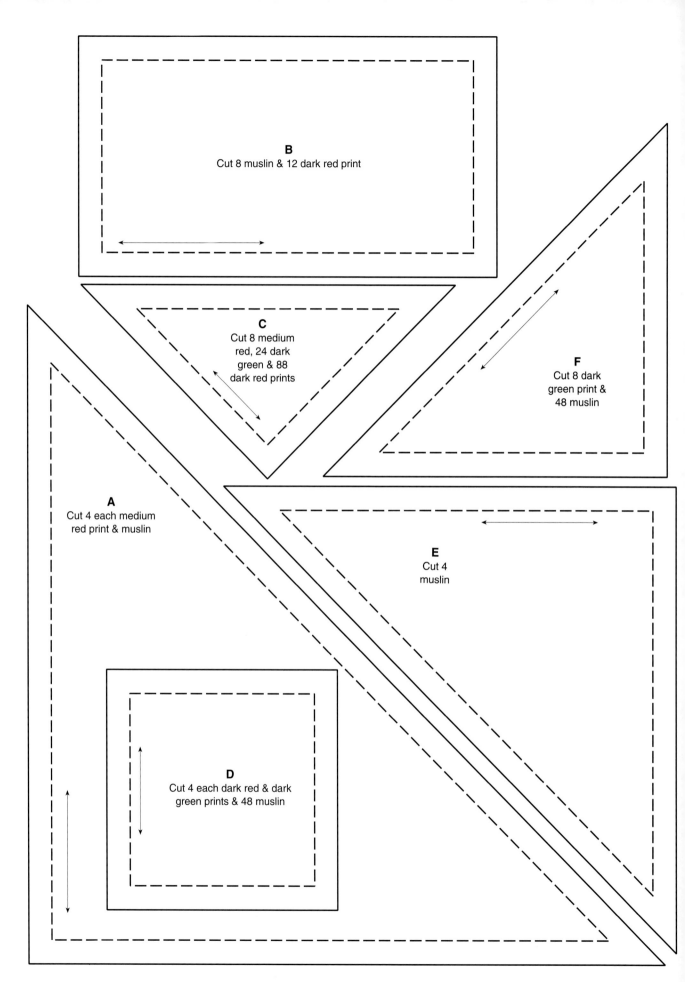

B
Cut 8 muslin & 12 dark red print

C
Cut 8 medium red, 24 dark green & 88 dark red prints

F
Cut 8 dark green print & 48 muslin

A
Cut 4 each medium red print & muslin

E
Cut 4 muslin

D
Cut 4 each dark red & dark green prints & 48 muslin

Patchwork in Winter

By Anne Dutton

Warm homes and the wonder of a snowflake during wintertime are memories evoked by this scrappy quilt. The appliqué shapes are sewn with a folk-art technique using pearl cotton, big stitches and pinked edges.

- **Skill Level:** Beginner
- **Quilt Size:** 37" x 43 1/2"
- **Block Size:** 3" x 3" and 6" x 6"
- **Number of Blocks:** 4 small and 5 large stars

- 3/4 yard cream print for center background
- 1/2 yard white print for snowflakes and snowmen
- 1/3 yard each dark green and tan prints for large pieced stars
- 1/4 yard navy star print for sky unit
- 1/4 yard gold mottled for small pieced and appliquéd stars
- 4 fat quarters coordinated fabrics for right border
- 1/4 yard winter print for left border
- 1/4 yard check print for inner border
- 6 1/2" x 14" rectangle green print
- Fat quarter each dark and light green prints for trees and shrubs
- Assorted scraps for cabin
- Scrap brown print for tree trunks
- Batting 41" x 48"
- Backing 41" x 48"
- Coordinating all-purpose thread
- 1 spool cream machine-quilting thread
- 1 ball white #8 pearl cotton
- Basic sewing supplies and tools, pinking shears and freezer paper

Patchwork in Winter
Placement Diagram
37" x 43 1/2"

Instructions

Step 1. Prepare templates using pattern pieces given; cut as directed on each piece for large and small stars. Cut all star, tree, shrub, snowman, snowflake and cabin appliqué pieces using pinking shears. **Note:** *Patterns list numbers to cut for separate designs.*

Step 2. To make one Small Star block, sew a gold mottled A to a navy star print A; repeat for four A-A units. Join these units with B squares to complete one block as shown in Figure 1; repeat for four blocks.

Step 3. Cut the following pieces from navy star

Figure 1
Arrange A-A units with B squares to complete a Small Star block.

print: one 1 1/2" x 7 1/2"; one 5 1/2" x 7 1/2"; one 1 1/2" x 3 1/2"; one 3 1/2" x 3 1/2"; one 8 1/2" x 7 1/2"; and three 3 1/2" x 4 1/2".

Step 4. Arrange the pieces cut in Step 3 with the four Small Star blocks as shown in Figure 2; join to complete sky unit.

1 1/2" x 3 1/2"

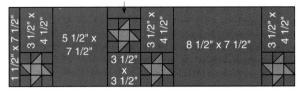

Figure 2
Arrange 4 Small Star blocks with rectangles, squares and strips as shown to complete sky unit.

Step 5. To make one Large Star block, sew a tan print C to a dark green print C; repeat for eight C-C units. Join C-C units with D and E squares to complete one block as shown in Figure 3; repeat for five blocks.

Figure 3
Join C-C units with D and E squares to make Large Star block.

Step 6. Cut a 22 1/2" x 26 1/2" rectangle cream print for center. Cut one strip 2 1/2" x 29 1/2" check print.

Step 7. Sew the sky unit to one 26 1/2" side of cream print rectangle; press seams toward sky unit. Sew the 2 1/2" x 29 1/2" check print strip to the left side of pieced center as shown in Figure 4; press seam

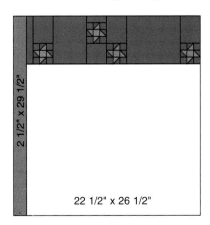

2 1/2" x 29 1/2"

22 1/2" x 26 1/2"

Figure 4
Sew the 2 1/2" x 29 1/2" strip to left side of the pieced center.

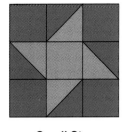

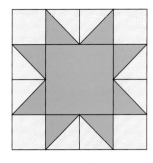

Small Star
3" x 3" Block

Large Star
6" x 6" Block

toward strip.

Step 8. Using all four coordinating fat quarter pieces, cut one of the following: 2" x 10"; 7" x 10"; 7 1/2" x 10"; and 14 1/2" x 10". Join these pieces to make a strip as shown in Figure 5. Sew the strip to the check-print side of the pieced center; press seams toward strips.

Step 9. Cut one strip check print 2 1/2" x 38"; sew to the bottom edge of the pieced center referring to Figure 6; press seam toward strip.

2" x 10"

7" x 10"

7 1/2" x 10"

14 1/2" x 10"

Figure 5
Join pieces to make a strip.

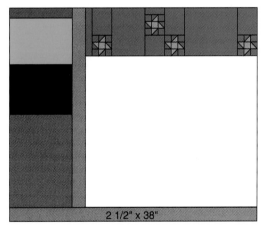

2 1/2" x 38"

Figure 6
Sew strip to bottom edge.

Step 10. Cut one strip winter print 6 1/2" x 31 1/2"; sew to the right side of the pieced section. Press seam toward strip.

Step 11. Join the five Large Star blocks to make a row. Sew the 6 1/2" x 14" green print rectangle to the left side of the pieced strip. Sew this strip to the bottom of the pieced center; press seams toward strip.

Step 12. To make trees and shrubs, sew a light green print C to a dark green print C; repeat for five units. Repeat with light and dark green print F pieces and light and dark green print G pieces for five units in each size. Repeat with the light and dark green print A pieces to make six A-A shrub units.

Step 13. Place a C-C unit on a dark green print scrap; pin. Using pinking shears, pink around the edges of the C-C unit, cutting a pinked-edge dark green print square at the same time. Repeat to make one each dark green print square with the F-F and G-G units.

Step 14. Referring to the Placement Diagram and Figure 7 for positioning, arrange and pin five C-C units with the C pinked-edge square on the pieced center to make small tree shape. Repeat with F-F units and square and G-G units and square to make medium and large tree shapes.

Figure 7
Arrange tree pieces as shown.

Step 15. Cut the following from brown print scrap for tree trunks: 1" x 9"; 3/4" x 6 1/2"; and 3/4" x 9". Pin these strips below tree shapes placing the 1" x 9" strip under the large tree, the 3/4" x 9" strip under the medium tree and the 3/4" x 6 1/2" strip under the small tree.

Step 16. Using pearl cotton and large stitches, hand-stitch around each shape about 1/8" in from edges all around.

Step 17. Place four gold mottled stars in the sky/background area referring to the Placement Diagram. Stitch in place as in Step 16.

Step 18. Arrange cabin pieces on cream print background area referring to Figure 8. Appliqué in place as in Step 16. Add A-A shrub units around bottom of cabin referring to the Placement Diagram.

Step 19. Arrange snowman pieces as shown in Figure 9 referring to the Placement Diagram for positioning. Stitch in place as in Step 16.

Step 20. To make snowflakes, cut six squares white print sized from 3" x 3" to 5" x 5". Iron freezer paper to the back of each square to stabilize for cutting.

Step 21. Fold one square in half and then in thirds as shown in Figure 10; using pinking shears, make cuts along each side of the folds and at the top point to form snowflakes. Repeat for remaining snowflakes.

Figure 10
Fold in thirds and
cut as shown.

Step 22. Remove freezer paper. Arrange snowflakes on pieced center referring to the Placement Diagram for positioning. Pin in place; stitch as in Step 16.

Step 23. Prepare for quilting and finish referring to General Instructions. ●

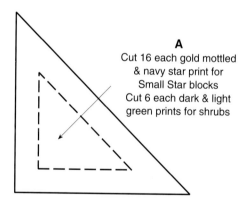

A
Cut 16 each gold mottled
& navy star print for
Small Star blocks
Cut 6 each dark & light
green prints for shrubs

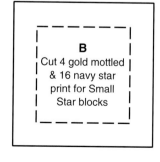

B
Cut 4 gold mottled
& 16 navy star
print for Small
Star blocks

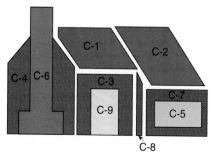

Figure 8
Arrange cabin shapes as shown.

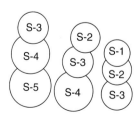

Figure 9
Arrange S pieces to make
snowmen as shown.

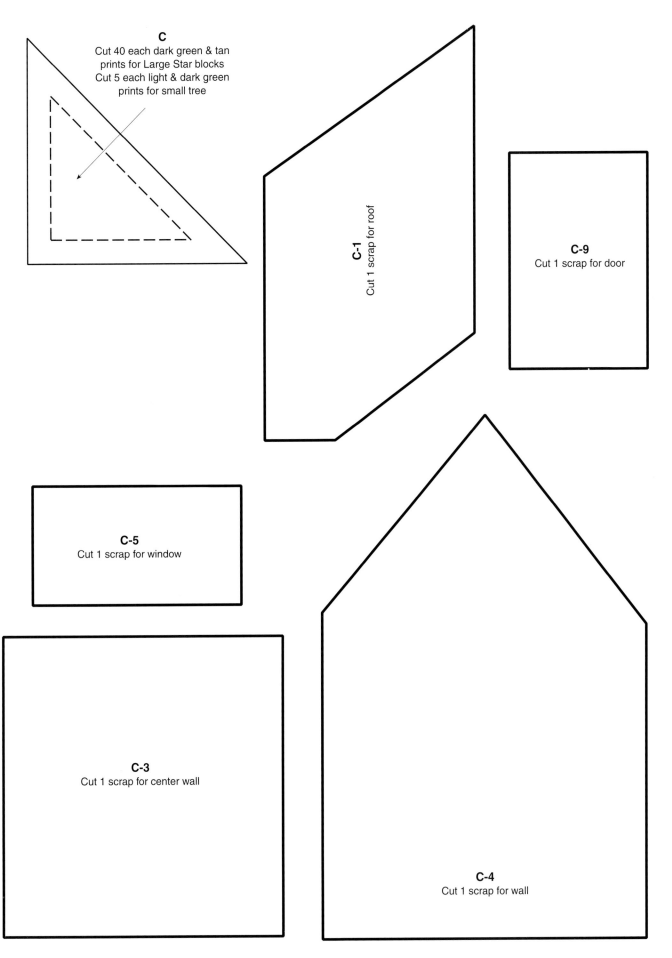

C
Cut 40 each dark green & tan
prints for Large Star blocks
Cut 5 each light & dark green
prints for small tree

C-1
Cut 1 scrap for roof

C-9
Cut 1 scrap for door

C-5
Cut 1 scrap for window

C-3
Cut 1 scrap for center wall

C-4
Cut 1 scrap for wall

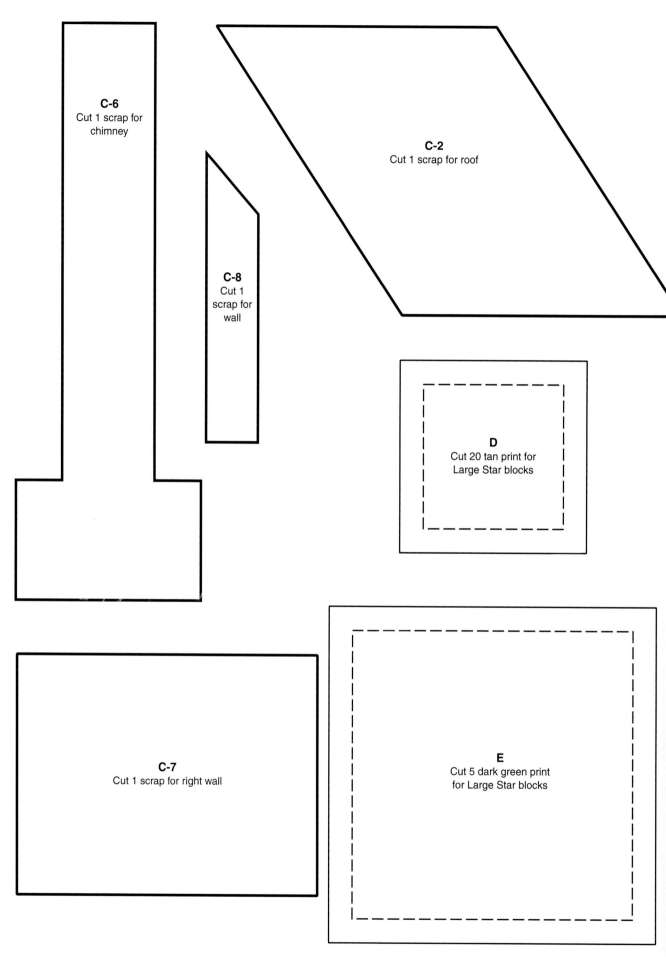

C-6
Cut 1 scrap for chimney

C-2
Cut 1 scrap for roof

C-8
Cut 1 scrap for wall

D
Cut 20 tan print for Large Star blocks

C-7
Cut 1 scrap for right wall

E
Cut 5 dark green print for Large Star blocks

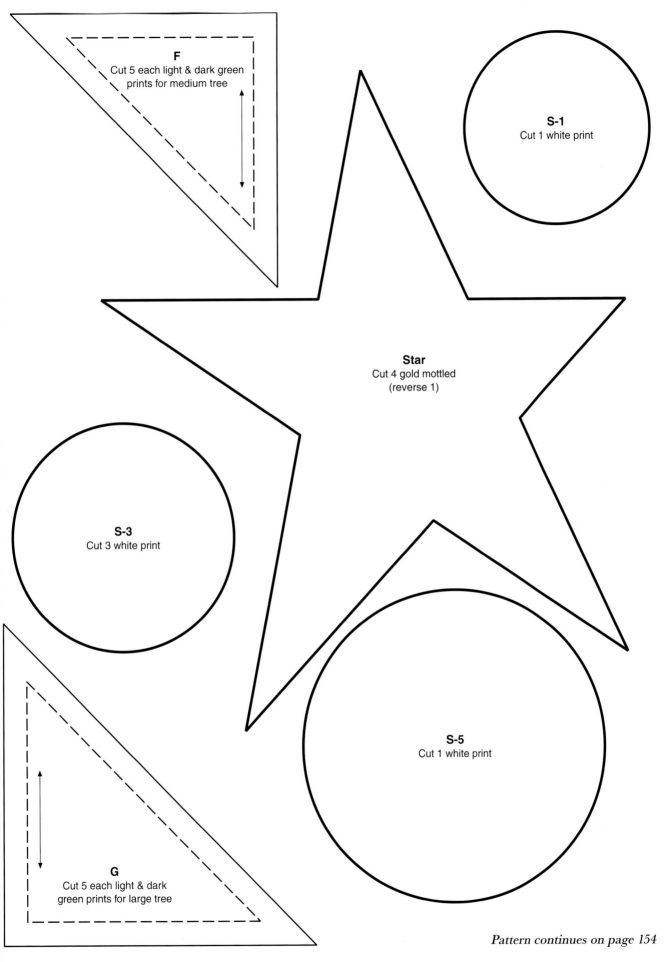

F
Cut 5 each light & dark green
prints for medium tree

S-1
Cut 1 white print

Star
Cut 4 gold mottled
(reverse 1)

S-3
Cut 3 white print

S-5
Cut 1 white print

G
Cut 5 each light & dark
green prints for large tree

Pattern continues on page 154

Peppermint Wheel

By Holly Daniels

S urround yourself with your favorite Christmas treat and don't gain an ounce when you make this fun quilt. It's the perfect excuse to use up some of your stash of red fabrics or splurge on a few new ones.

Peppermint Wheels
Placement Diagram
70" x 84"

- **Skill Level:** Intermediate
- **Quilt Size:** 70" x 84"
- **Block Size:** 12" x 12"
- **Number of Blocks:** 20

- 1/3 yard each 20 different red prints
- 1/4 yard green print
- 3/4 yard total green scraps
- 2 1/2 yards white-on-white print
- Batting 74" x 88"
- Backing 74" x 88"
- 9 yards self-made or purchased binding
- All-purpose thread to match fabrics
- Basic sewing supplies and tools

Instructions

Step 1. Cut two strips each 2 1/2" x 58 1/2" and 2 1/2" x 72 1/2" white-on-white print along length of fabric for border strips; set aside.

Step 2. Cut seven strips 4 7/8" x 32" across remaining width of white-on-white print; cut into 4 7/8" square segments. Cut seven strips 2 1/2" x 32" across remaining width of white-on-white print; cut into 2 1/2" square segments.

Step 3. Cut one strip from each of the red prints 2 1/2" by fabric width. Cut into two 8 1/2" and two 12 1/2" segments. Cut two 4 7/8" x 4 7/8" squares from each red print.

Step 4. Cut all red print and white-on-white print 4 7/8" x 4 7/8" squares in half on one diagonal to make triangles. You will need 80 white-on-white print and four each of the 20 different red print triangles.

Step 5. To piece one block, sew a red print triangle to a white-on-white print triangle as shown in Figure 1; repeat for four same-print units; press seams toward red print triangles.

Step 6. Join four same-print triangle units to make a pinwheel unit as shown in Figure 2; press seams in one direction.

Figure 1
Sew a white-on-white print triangle to a red print triangle.

Figure 2
Join 4 same-print units to make a pinwheel unit.

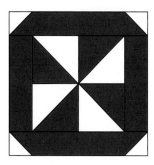

Peppermint Wheels
12" x 12" Block

Step 7. Sew a same-print 2 1/2" x 8 1/2" rectangle to opposite sides of the pieced pinwheel unit as shown in Figure 3; press seams toward rectangles.

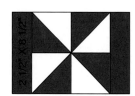

Figure 3
Sew a 2 1/2" x 8 1/2" strip
to opposite sides of the
pinwheel unit.

Step 8. Place a 2 1/2" x 2 1/2" white-on-white print square on each end of a same-print 2 1/2" x 12 1/2" rectangle. Sew across diagonal of squares referring to Figure 4 for direction to stitch. Press back over seams; trim excess as shown in Figure 5; repeat for two units. Sew to remaining sides of the pinwheel unit as shown in Figure 6 to complete one block; repeat for 20 blocks.

2 1/2" x 2 1/2"

2 1/2" x 12 1/2"

Figure 4
Sew on the diagonals of the squares as shown.

Figure 5
Trim excess as shown.

Figure 6
Sew to the pieced unit
to complete 1 block.

Step 9. Cut 49 strips white-on-white print 2 1/2" x 12 1/2" for sashing. Cut 30 squares green print

2 1/2" x 2 1/2" for sashing squares.

Step 10. Join four blocks with five 2 1/2" x 12 1/2" sashing strips to make a block row as shown in Figure 7; repeat for five rows. Press seams toward sashing strips.

2 1/2" x 12 1/2"

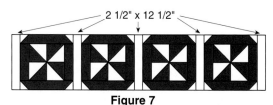

Figure 7
Join 4 blocks with 5 sashing strips to make a block row.

Step 11. Join five green print squares with four sashing strips to make a sashing row as shown in Figure 8; repeat for six rows. Press seams toward sashing strips.

2 1/2" x 2 1/2"   2 1/2" x 12 1/2"

Figure 8
Join 5 sashing squares with 4 sashing strips to make a sashing row.

Step 12. Join sashing rows with block rows beginning and ending with a sashing row to complete pieced center; press seams toward sashing rows.

Step 13. To make border strips, cut four squares of one red print 6 1/2" x 6 1/2"; set aside. Cut green scraps and remaining red fabrics into 2 1/2" x 4 1/2" segments. You will need 64 red and 68 green segments. Join 29 segments, beginning with green and alternating red and green, to make a strip; repeat. Press seams in one direction. Sew a 2 1/2" x 58 1/2" strip white-on-white print to one side of each strip referring to Figure 9; press seams toward white-on-white print. Sew a strip to the top and bottom of the pieced center.

2 1/2" x 58 1/2"

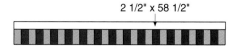

Figure 9
Sew a 2 1/2" x 58 1/2" white-on-white
print strip to 1 side of the pieced strip.

Step 14. Join 37 segments, beginning with green and alternating red and green, to make a strip; repeat. Center and sew a 2 1/2" x 72 1/2" strip white-on-white print to one side of each strip; press seams toward white-on-white print. Trim pieced strip ends even with white-on-white print strip.

Step 15. Sew a 6 1/2" x 6 1/2" red print square to each end of each strip; press seams toward squares. Sew a strip to the remaining long sides; press seams toward strips.

Step 16. Prepare for quilting and finish referring to General Instructions. ●

Strips & Stripes

By Holly Daniels

ig out all your red fabrics to make a scrappy-looking quilt that is both quick and easy.

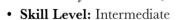

- **Skill Level:** Intermediate
- **Quilt Size:** Approximately 80" x 94"
- **Block Size:** 9 1/2" x 9 1/2"
- **Number of Blocks:** 20 Stripe and 30 Nine-Patch

- 3 yards green print
- 2 1/4 yards beige print
- 6 yards total dark red scraps
- Batting 84" x 98"
- Backing 84" x 98"
- 11 yards self-made or purchased binding
- All-purpose thread to match fabrics
- Basic sewing supplies and tools

Strips & Stripes
Placement Diagram
Approximately 80" x 94"

Instructions

Step 1. Cut 10 strips green print and eight strips beige print 2 3/4" by fabric width. Sew a beige print strip between two green print strips; repeat for four strip sets. Sew a green print strip between two beige print strips; repeat for two strip sets.

Step 2. Cut each strip set into 2 3/4" segments as shown in Figure 1. You will need 60 green/beige/green and 30

beige/green/beige segments.

Step 3. Sew a beige/green/beige segment between two green/beige/green segments to make a Nine-Patch unit as shown in Figure 2; repeat for 30 units.

Step 4. Cut nine strips beige print 5 3/4" by fabric width. Cut each strip into 5 3/4" square segments; you will need 60 squares. Cut each square in half on one diagonal to make two triangles; you will need 120 triangles.

Step 5. Sew a triangle to each side of a Nine-Patch unit to complete one Nine-Patch block as shown in Figure 3. Press seams toward triangles; trim to 10" x 10" squares, if necessary.

Step 6. Prepare templates for pieces A–F using pattern pieces given, referring to Figure 4 for A and B templates. Cut as directed on each piece. **Note:** *If you are able to cut strips from your dark red fabric, cut strips 2 3/4" wide; lay templates A, B, D and E on strips as shown in Figure 5 to save time in cutting.*

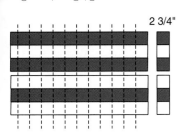

2 3/4"

Figure 1
Cut strips into 2 3/4" segments.

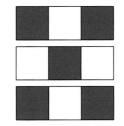

Figure 2
Join segments as shown to make a Nine-Patch unit.

Figure 3
Sew a triangle to each side
of a Nine-Patch unit to
complete 1 block.

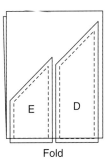
Fold
Figure 4
Place templates D
and E on fold of
template material
to make templates
A and B as shown.

Figure 5
Place template on strip as shown.

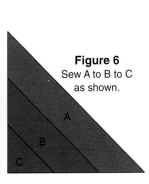

Figure 6
Sew A to B to C
as shown.

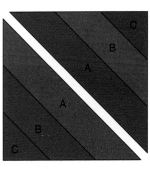

Figure 7
Join 2 A-B-C units to complete
Stripe block as shown.

Step 7. Sew A to B to C as shown in Figure 6; press seams away from A. Repeat for 40 units. Join two units as shown in Figure 7 to complete one Stripe block; repeat for 20 blocks. Trim to 10" x 10" squares, if necessary.

Step 8. Sew D to E to F and DR to ER to F; press seams away from D. Repeat for 80 units. Join two units as shown in Figure 8 to make side fill-in triangles.

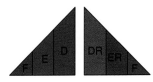

Figure 8
Join units as shown to make
side fill-in triangles.

Step 9. Cut two squares 7 5/8" x 7 5/8" from red scraps. Cut each square in half on one diagonal to make corner triangles.

Step 10. Arrange blocks in diagonal rows, adding 18 side fill-in and four corner triangles as shown in

Figure 9
Join blocks in diagonal rows with
side fill-in and corner triangles.

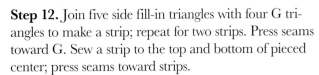

Figure 10
Join 6 side fill-in
triangles with 5 G
triangles to make
long border strips
for sides.

Figure 9. Join in rows; join rows to complete pieced center. Press seams in one direction.

Step 11. Cut five squares green print 14 5/8" x 14 5/8". Cut each square on both diagonals to make G triangles. Join six side fill-in triangles with five G triangles to make a strip as shown in Figure 10; repeat for two strips. Press seams toward G. Sew a strip to opposite long sides of pieced center; press seams toward strips.

Step 12. Join five side fill-in triangles with four G triangles to make a strip; repeat for two strips. Press seams toward G. Sew a strip to the top and bottom of pieced center; press seams toward strips.

Step 13. Cut six squares green print 7 5/8" x 7 5/8". Cut each square in half on one diagonal to make H triangles. Join three H triangles as shown in Figure 11; repeat for four units. Sew an H unit to each corner of the quilt top; press seams toward H units.

Figure 11
Join 3 H pieces
as shown.

Step 14. Prepare for quilting and finish referring to General Instructions. ●

Nine-Patch
9 1/2" x 9 1/2" Block

Stripe
9 1/2" x 9 1/2" Block

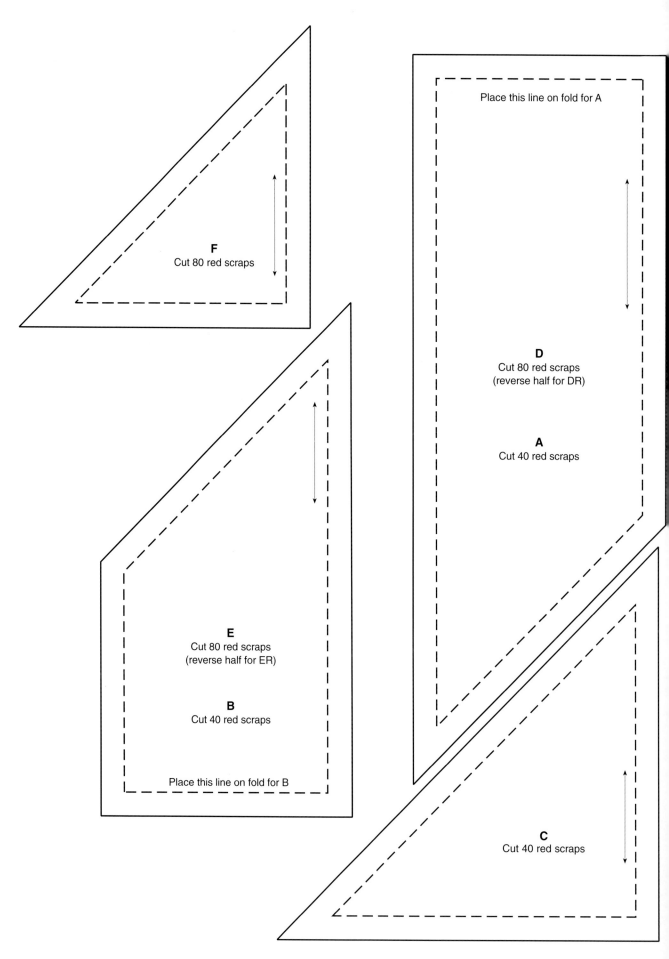

F
Cut 80 red scraps

Place this line on fold for A

D
Cut 80 red scraps
(reverse half for DR)

A
Cut 40 red scraps

E
Cut 80 red scraps
(reverse half for ER)

B
Cut 40 red scraps

Place this line on fold for B

C
Cut 40 red scraps

Christmas is Love

By Eileen Westfall

he message is simple and obvious. The spirit of love is in the air during the Christmas season.

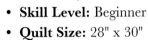

- **Skill Level:** Beginner
- **Quilt Size:** 28" x 30"
- **Block Size:** 4" x 4" and 8" x 8"
- **Number of Blocks:** 12 Heart, 10 Four-Patch and 4 Tree/Heart

- 1/8 yard each red solid and very dark green print
- 1/4 yard each dark green print, white solid, red plaid, red print and green check
- 5/8 yard light green print
- Batting 32" x 34"
- Backing 32" x 34"
- 3 1/2 yards self-made or purchased binding
- Coordinating all-purpose thread
- White quilting thread
- Green 6-strand embroidery floss
- Basic sewing supplies and tools and disappearing fabric marker

Christmas Is Love
Placement Diagram
28" x 30"

Four-Patch
4" x 4" Block

Heart
4" x 4" Block

Tree/Heart
8" x 8" Block

Instructions

Step 1. Prepare templates using pattern pieces given; cut as directed on each piece, adding seam allowance for hand applique.

Step 2. Hand-appliqué one red solid heart to each tree shape referring to tree pattern for positioning of heart.

Step 3. Cut four squares light green print 8 1/2" x 8 1/2". Center a tree/heart shape on each square; hand-appliqué in place.

Step 4. Join two blocks to make a row; repeat. Press seams in one direction. Join the two rows to complete center section.

Step 5. Cut two strips each red print 1 1/2" x 16 1/2" and 1 1/2" x 18 1/2". Sew the shorter strips to the top and bottom and longer strips to opposite sides; press seams toward strips.

Step 6. Cut one strip white solid 2 1/2" x 18 1/2"; sew to the top of the pieced unit; press seam toward red print strip. Center and trace letters for message onto strip using disappearing fabric marker. Using 4 strands green embroidery floss and a backstitch, embroider each letter.

Step 7. Cut 12 squares light green print 4 1/2" x 4 1/2".

Center and hand-appliqué a white solid heart to eight of the squares. Center a very dark green print heart diagonally on the four remaining light green print squares referring to Figure 1. Hand-appliqué in place.

Figure 1
Place heart on square
on the diagonal.

Figure 2
Join 2 units to make a
Four-Patch block.

Step 8. Cut 20 squares each red plaid and green check 2 1/2" x 2 1/2". Sew a red plaid square to a green plaid square; repeat for 20 units. Join two units as shown in Figure 2 to make a Four-Patch block; repeat for 10 blocks.

Step 9. Cut two rectangles red plaid 2 1/2" x 4 1/2". Arrange and stitch two Four-Patch blocks with two white solid heart blocks and a red plaid rectangle to make a row as shown in Figure 3; repeat for two rows. Press seams in one direction. Sew a row to the top and bottom of the pieced center; press seams toward strips.

21/2" x 4 1/2"

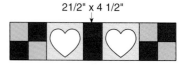

Figure 3
Join blocks with 2 1/2" x 4 1/2"
rectangle to make a row.

Step 10. Arrange and stitch three Four-Patch blocks with two white solid heart blocks and two very dark green heart blocks to make a row as shown in Figure 4; repeat for two rows. Press seams in one direction. Sew a row to opposite sides of the pieced center; press seams toward strips.

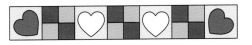

Figure 4
Join blocks to make a row.

Step 11. Cut two strips each red print 1 1/2" x 26 1/2" and 1 1/2" x 30 1/2". Sew the shorter strips to the top and bottom and longer strips to opposite sides; press seams toward strips.

Step 12. Prepare for quilting and finish referring to General Instructions. ●

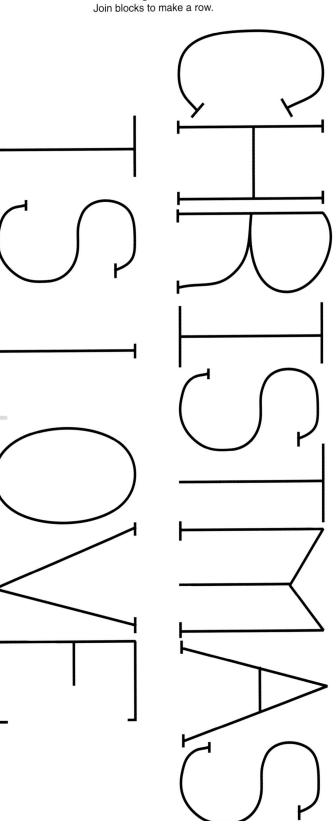

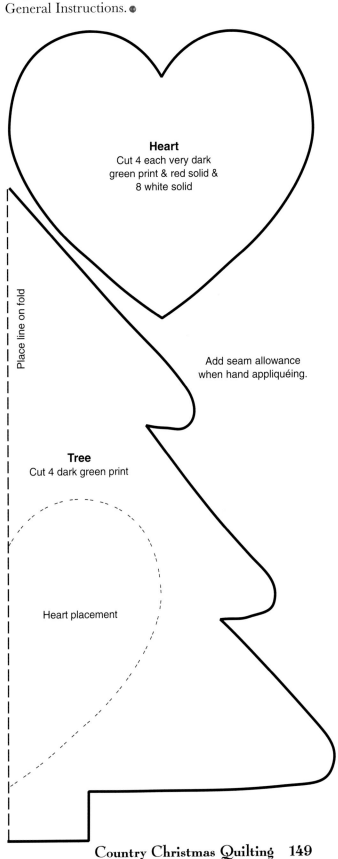

Heart
Cut 4 each very dark green print & red solid & 8 white solid

Add seam allowance when hand appliquéing.

Place line on fold

Tree
Cut 4 dark green print

Heart placement

The Perfect Tree

By Carla Schwab

If you have a live tree every year, you probably search for that perfect one—you know the shape and size you like. This quilt has one perfect tree. Can you find it?

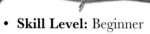

- **Skill Level:** Beginner
- **Quilt Size:** 52" x 59"
- **Block Size:** 7" x 7"
- **Number of Blocks:** 9 Road to California and 33 Tree blocks

- 1/4 yard each tan and brown prints
- 1/4 yard each of 8 different green prints
- 1 1/4 yards green print for borders and blocks
- 1 1/2 yards white-on-off-white print
- 3" x 3" scrap gold solid
- Batting 56" x 63"
- Backing 56" x 63"
- 6 1/2 yards self-made or purchased binding
- Coordinating all-purpose thread
- White quilting thread
- Gold 6-strand embroidery floss
- Basic sewing supplies and tools

Instructions

Step 1. Prepare templates using pattern pieces given; cut as directed on each piece.

Step 2. To piece one Tree block, sew D and DR to C as shown in Figure 1; press seams toward C. Repeat for 33 blocks.

Figure 1
Sew D and DR to C to
make a Tree block.

Figure 2
Join A-A units with B to make
a Road to California block.

Step 3. To piece one Road to California block, sew a brown print A to a white-on-off-white print A; repeat for four units. Arrange A-A units with B squares as shown in Figure 2; press seams in one direction. Repeat for nine blocks.

Step 4. Lay out blocks in seven rows of six blocks each referring to the Placement Diagram for positioning of Road to California blocks. Join blocks in rows; join rows to complete pieced center. Press seams in one direction.

Step 5. Cut two strips each green print 5 1/2" x 49 1/2" and 5 1/2" x 52 1/2". Sew the shorter strips to opposite sides and longer strips to top and bottom; press seams toward strips.

Step 6. Choose your perfect tree. Using 3 strands of gold embroidery floss and a blanket stitch, hand-appliqué star in place at treetop.

Step 7. Mark Leaf Quilting Design on border strips as shown in Figure 3. Sandwich batting between pieced top and prepared backing; pin or baste to hold. Quilt border strips and as desired using white quilting thread; remove pins. Trim edges even.

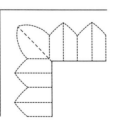 

Figure 3
Mark quilting design
on border as shown.

Figure 4
Place pattern on corner
edge as shown.

Step 8. Prepare template for Corner Pattern. Place on edge of one corner as shown in Figure 4; trace pattern on edge. Flip pattern; place on adjacent corner edge and trace. Trim on traced line through all layers. Repeat on each corner.

Step 9. Finish edges referring to General Instructions. ❧

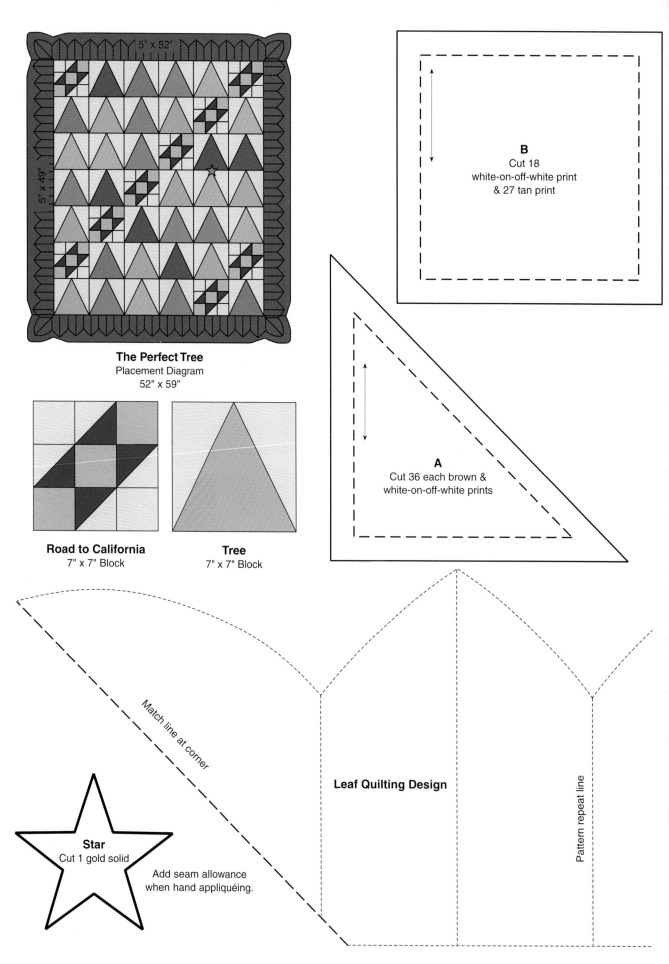

The Perfect Tree
Placement Diagram
52" x 59"

Road to California
7" x 7" Block

Tree
7" x 7" Block

B
Cut 18
white-on-off-white print
& 27 tan print

A
Cut 36 each brown &
white-on-off-white prints

Match line at corner

Leaf Quilting Design

Pattern repeat line

Star
Cut 1 gold solid

Add seam allowance
when hand appliquéing.

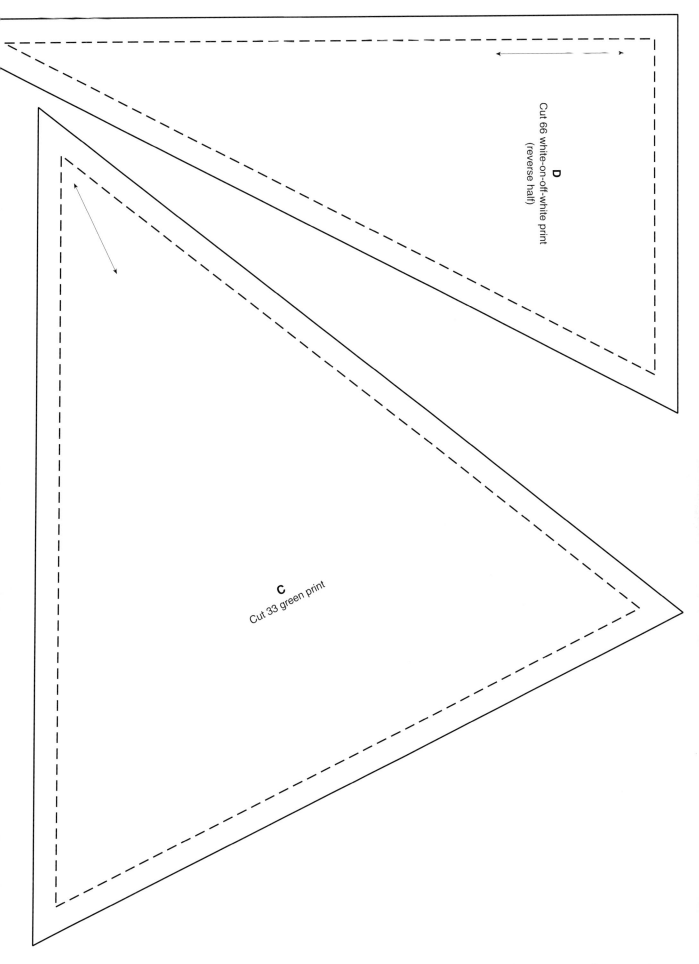

D
Cut 66 white-on-off-white print
(reverse half)

C
Cut 33 green print

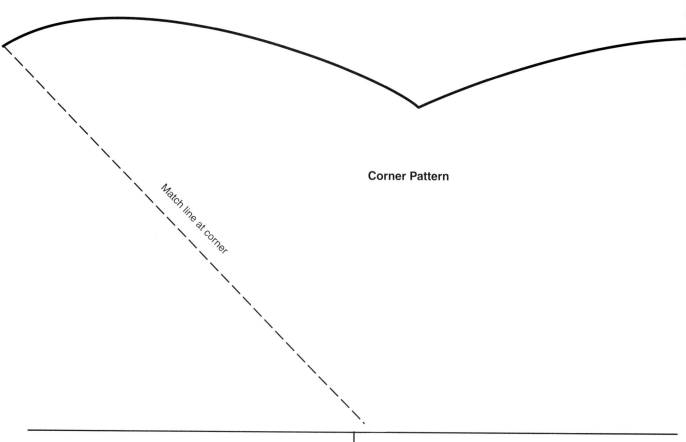

Corner Pattern

Match line at corner

Holiday Village

Continued from page 125

Step 4. Cut two strips off-white print 2 1/2" x 32 1/2"; sew a strip to opposite long sides. Press seams toward strips.

Step 5. Cut one strip each blue and off-white prints 2 1/2" by fabric width. Sew strips together along length; press seams toward blue print. Subcut into eight 2 1/2" segments.

Step 6. Join two blue/off-white segments to make a Four-Patch block as shown in Figure 8; repeat for four blocks.

Figure 8
Join 2 segments to make a Four-Patch block.

Step 7. Cut two strips burgundy print 4 1/2" x 24 1/2"; sew to top and bottom of pieced center. Press seams toward strips. Cut two strips burgundy print 4 1/2" x 32 1/2". Sew a Four-Patch block to each end of each strip; press seams toward blocks. Sew a strip to opposite sides of pieced center; press seams toward strips.

Step 8. Prepare for quilting and finish referring to General Instructions.

Step 9. Sew a gold wooden star button to the top of each tree block with off-white linen thread to finish. ●

Patchwork in Winter

Continued from page 139

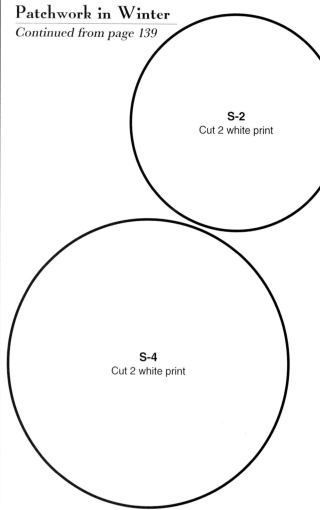

S-2
Cut 2 white print

S-4
Cut 2 white print

Blue Christmas

By Connie Rand

You may think the title of this quilt is rather melancholy, but it refers to the color scheme of the quilt, not to a depressed mental state!

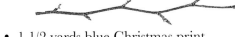

- **Skill Level:** Advanced
- **Project Size:** 77" x 101"
- **Block Size:** 12" x 12"
- **Number of Blocks:** 48

- 1 1/2 yards blue Christmas print
- 3 yards light blue print
- 2 1/4 yards dark blue print
- 1 yard dark blue solid
- 1 yard muslin
- Backing 81" x 105"
- Batting 81" x 105"
- 10 yards self-made or purchased binding
- Neutral color all-purpose thread
- Basic sewing supplies and tools

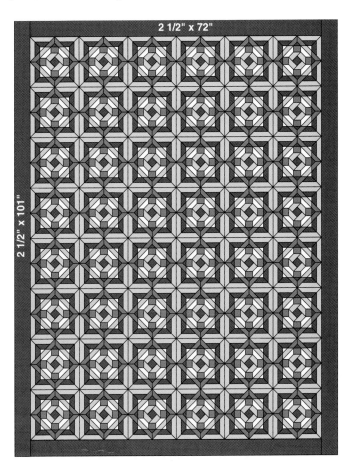

Blue Christmas
Placement Diagram
77" x 101"

Instructions

Step 1. Cut and piece two strips 3" x 101 1/2" and two strips 3" x 72 1/2" dark blue solid. Set aside for borders.

Step 2. Prepare templates using pattern pieces given. Cut as directed on each piece for one block.

Step 3. Sew B to A, stop-

ping at the end of the A seam line as shown in Figure 1.

Step 4. Add remaining B pieces; finish sewing first seam to complete A-B unit as shown in Figure 2; press seam toward B. Add C pieces again referring to Figure 2. Set in a muslin D between C pieces; add dark blue print E as shown in Figure 3 to complete the block center unit.

Figure 1
Sew B to A, starting and stopping at ends of A seam line.

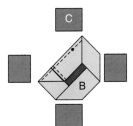

Figure 2
Complete first A-B seam as shown; add C.

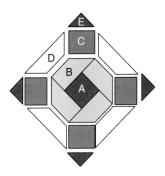

Figure 3
Set in muslin D; add dark blue E.

Step 5. Sew F to each side of a light blue print D as shown in Figure 4. Repeat for four F-D-F units; press.

Figure 4
Sew F to each side of light
blue print D as shown.

Step 6. Sew G to H; repeat for eight G-H units. Join two G-H units; set in a muslin E as shown in Figure 5. Repeat for four E-G-H units; press.

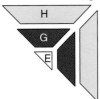

Figure 5
Sew G to H; repeat. Join
and set in E as shown.

Step 7. Sew an F-D-F unit to an E-G-H unit to complete one block corner unit; repeat for four block corner units.

Step 8. Join the block center and block corner units as shown in Figure 6 to complete one block; repeat for 48 blocks.

Step 9. Join six blocks to complete one row; repeat for eight rows. Join rows to complete pieced center; press.

Step 10. Sew the 3" x 72 1/2" dark blue solid strips to the top and bottom of the pieced center; press seams toward strips.

Step 11. Sew the 3" x 101 1/2" dark blue solid strips to the remaining sides; press seams toward strips.

Step 12. Prepare pieced top for quilting and finish referring to General Instructions. ●

Figure 6
Join units as shown to complete 1 block.

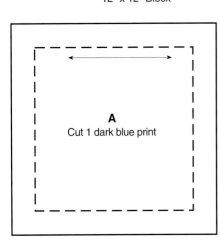

Blue Christmas
12" x 12" Block

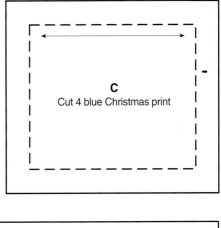

C
Cut 4 blue Christmas print

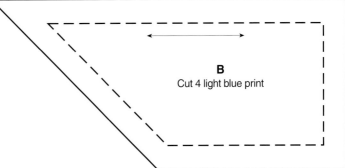

A
Cut 1 dark blue print

B
Cut 4 light blue print

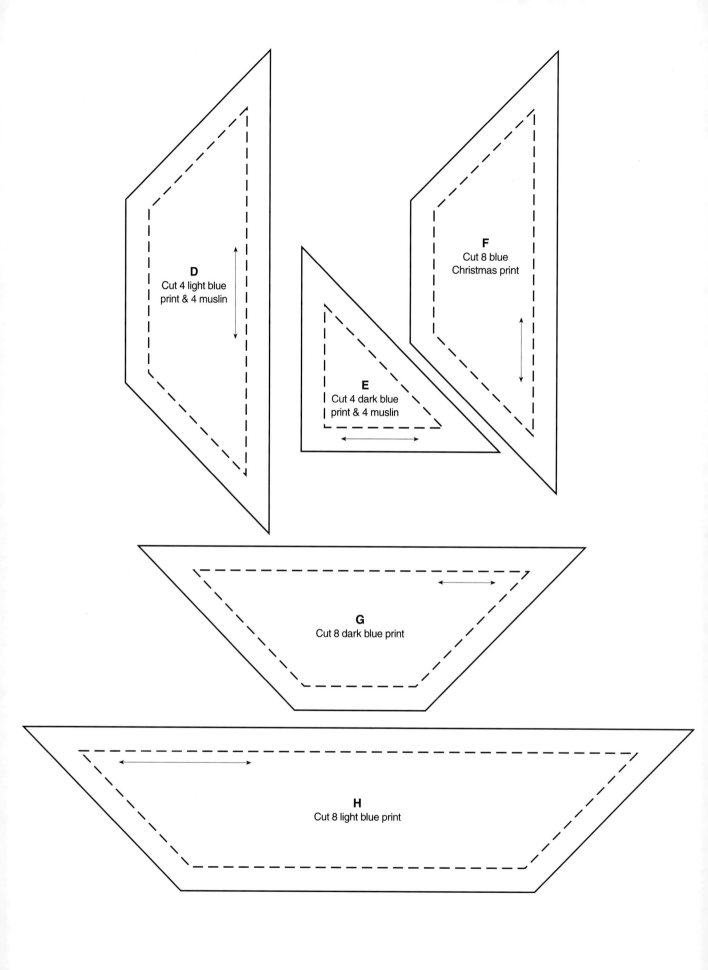

D
Cut 4 light blue
print & 4 muslin

F
Cut 8 blue
Christmas print

E
Cut 4 dark blue
print & 4 muslin

G
Cut 8 dark blue print

H
Cut 8 light blue print

Fiesta Stars

By Lucy A. Fazely

F oundation piecing makes sewing the narrow points of the star designs accurate and easy. Repeat the colors of the stars in the borders to make an elegant decorator quilt.

- **Skill Level:** Intermediate
- **Quilt Size:** 52 1/8" x 52 1/8"
- **Block Size:** 8" x 8"
- **Number of Blocks:** 13

- 1/8 yard each dark red and dark purple prints for center star
- 1/8 yard each 2 medium red prints for outside stars
- 1/8 yard each 2 medium purple prints for outside stars
- 5/8 yard beige print
- 1 1/4 yards off-white print
- 1 5/8 yards border print
- Backing 56" x 56"
- Batting 56" x 56"
- 6 yards self-made or purchased binding
- Coordinating all-purpose thread
- 2 yards fabric stabilizer
- Basic sewing supplies and tools

Project Notes

Tear-off fabric stabilizer is used as the foundation for paper-piecing blocks. You may substitute muslin, copy paper or tracing paper. For best sewing results, use a 90/14 needle and set your machine for 18–20 stitches per inch.

Instructions

Step 1. Press fabric stabilizer; cut into sections 1" larger than each block needed for foundation piecing—for a 4" x 4" block, cut a 5" x 5" square stabilizer.

Step 2. Center stabilizer over drawing for Block A; trace lines onto stabilizer using a ruler and pencil. Mark the numbers in each area. Draw a 1/4" seam allowance around the drawn design.

Step 3. Turn the stabilizer square over; mark the colors needed for each area on this side. ***Note: This is the right side of the block.*** Repeat for four each A, B, C, E and F blocks and eight D blocks.

Step 4. Cut fabric pieces in colors needed 1" larger than the space drawn on the stabilizer. Lay piece 1 on the stabilizer over the space marked 1 with the

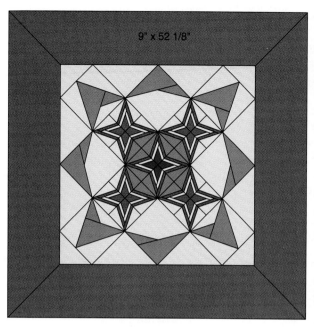

Fiesta Stars
Placement Diagram
52 1/8" x 52 1/8"

wrong side of the fabric patch on the unlined side of the stabilizer. ***Note: You should be able to see the lines marked on the wrong side of the stabilizer.*** Place piece 2 on top of piece 1 with right sides together. Pin along the line between pieces 1 and 2 as shown in Figure 1. Fold piece 2 over at pin to check that it generously covers the area marked 2.

Figure 1
Pin piece 2 right sides together
with piece 1 along marked line on
other side of stabilizer square.

Step 5. Remove pin; pin again away from the line. Stitch along line, extending stitching 1/8" before and after the line. Turn piece over; trim seam allowance to 1/4". Press piece 2 flat. Continue adding pieces in numerical order using the same procedure until stabilizer block is covered.

Step 6. Trim fabric to the outside line drawn on the stabilizer block. Repeat to make all blocks as indicated in Step 3. Do not remove stabilizer at this time.

Step 7. Join four A blocks to make center star block as shown in Figure 2. Press and square up to 8 1/2" x 8 1/2", if necessary.

Figure 2
Join 4 A blocks to make
the center star block.

Figure 3
Join B, C and D blocks to
make a Fiesta Star block.

Step 8. Join B, C and D blocks to make a Fiesta Star block as shown in Figure 3; repeat for four blocks. Press and square up to 8 1/2" x 8 1/2", if necessary.

Step 9. Cut two squares each 6 1/2" x 6 1/2" and 12 1/2" x 12 1/2" off-white print.

Step 10. Cut each 6 1/2" x 6 1/2" square in half on one diagonal to make X corner triangles. Cut each 12 1/2" x 12 1/2" square in half on both diagonals to make Z side fill-in triangles.

Step 11. Lay out star blocks with E and F blocks and the X and Z triangles referring to Figure 4. Join in diagonal rows; join rows to complete pieced top.

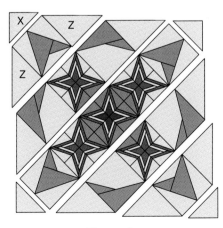

Figure 4
Lay out blocks and triangles as shown;
sew together in diagonal rows.

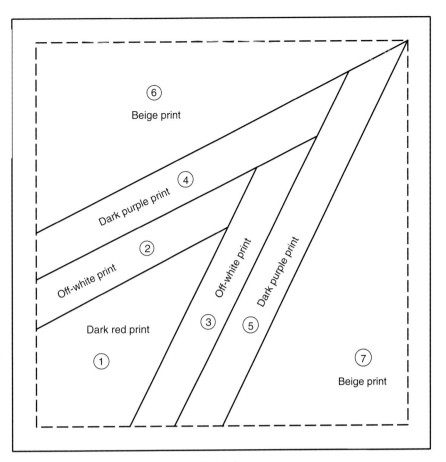

Block A
Make 4

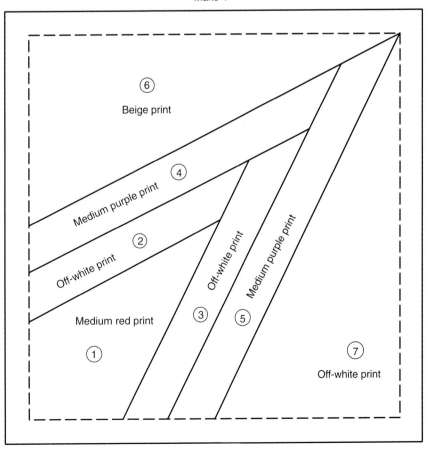

Block B
Make 4

Block A
Make 4

Block B
Make 4

Block C
Make 4

Block D
Make 8

Block E
Make 4

Block F
Make 4

Fiesta Star
8" x 8" Block

Step 12. Cut four strips border print 9 1/2" x 52 5/8" along length of border stripe. Fold each strip crosswise to mark center; crease. **Note:** *The width of the strip could vary depending on the width of the border design on your fabric. It is important to cut four identical border strips so that corners make the same design after mitering, as illustrated in photograph of quilt.*

Step 13. Sew a strip to each side of the pieced center, matching center crease on strips to side centers of pieced center. Miter corners referring to General Instructions; trim excess and press.

Step 14. Prepare quilt for quilting and finish as in General Instructions, binding edges with self-made or purchased binding. ●

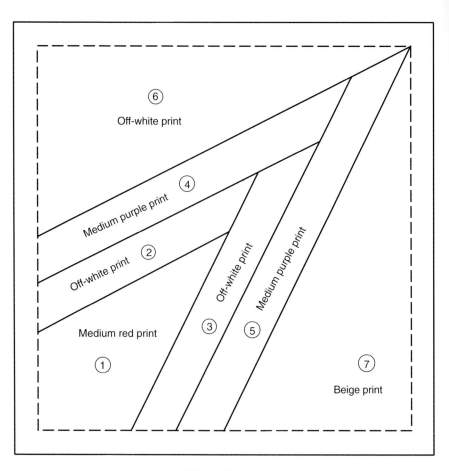

Off-white print ⑥

Medium purple print ④

Off-white print ②

Off-white print ③

Medium purple print ⑤

Medium red print ①

Beige print ⑦

Block C
Make 4

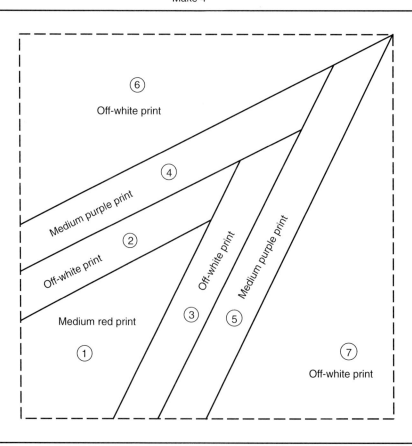

Off-white print ⑥

Medium purple print ④

Off-white print ②

Off-white print ③

Medium purple print ⑤

Medium red print ①

Off-white print ⑦

Block D
Make 8

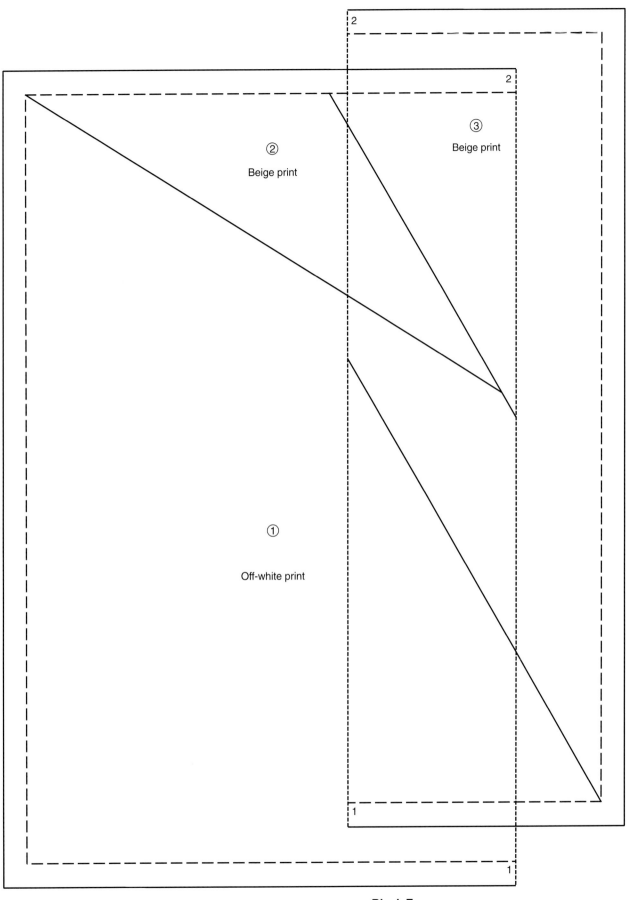

②
Beige print

③
Beige print

①
Off-white print

Block E
Make 4

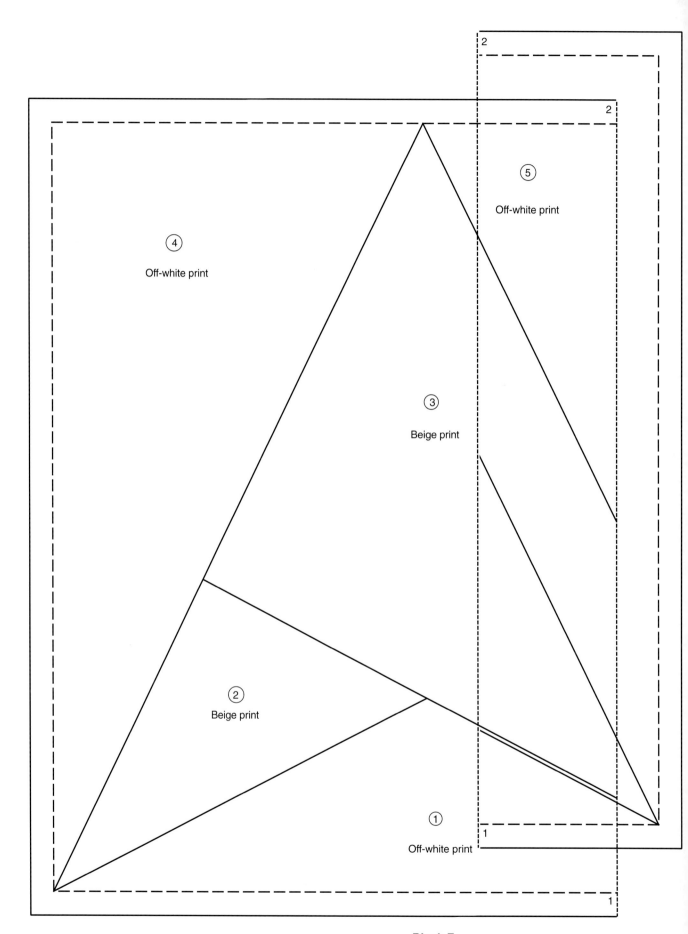

Block F
Make 4

Quiltmaking Basics

Materials & Supplies

Fabrics

Fabric Choices. Christmas quilts and projects combine fabrics of many types, depending on the project. It is best to combine same-fiber-content fabrics when making quilted items.

Buying Fabrics. One hundred percent cotton fabrics are recommended for making quilts. Choose colors similar to those used in the quilts shown or colors of your own preference. Most quilt designs depend more on contrast of values than on the colors used to create the design.

Preparing the Fabric for Use. Fabrics may be prewashed or not depending on your preference. Whether you do or don't, be sure your fabrics are colorfast and won't run onto each other when washed after use.

Fabric Grain. Fabrics are woven with threads going in a crosswise and lengthwise direction. The threads cross at right angles—the more threads per inch, the stronger the fabric.

The crosswise threads will stretch a little. The lengthwise threads will not stretch at all. Cutting the fabric at a 45-degree angle to the crosswise and lengthwise threads produces a bias edge which stretches a great deal when pulled (Figure 1).

If templates are given with patterns in this book, pay careful attention to the grain lines marked with arrows. These arrows indicate that the piece should be placed on the lengthwise grain with the arrow running on one thread. Although it is not necessary to examine the fabric and find a thread to match to, it is important to try to place the arrow with the lengthwise grain of the fabric (Figure 2).

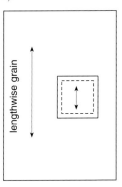

Figure 2
Place the template with marked arrow on the lengthwise grain of the fabric.

Thread

For most piecing, good-quality cotton or cotton-covered polyester is the thread of choice. Inexpensive polyester threads are not recommended because they can cut the fibers of cotton fabrics.

Choose a color thread that will match or blend with the fabrics in your quilt. For projects pieced with dark and light color fabrics choose a neutral thread color, such as a medium gray, as a compromise between colors. Test by pulling a sample seam.

Batting

Batting is the material used to give a quilt loft or thickness. It also adds warmth.

Batting size is listed in inches for each pattern to reflect the size needed to complete the quilt according to the instructions. Purchase the size large enough to cut the size you need for the quilt of your choice.

Some qualities to look for in batting are drapeability, resistance to fiber migration, loft and softness.

If you are unsure which kind of batting to use, purchase the smallest size batting available in the type you'd like to try. Test each sample on a small project. Choose the batting that you like working with most and that will result in the type of quilt you need.

Tools & Equipment

There are few truly essential tools and little equipment required for quiltmaking. The basics include needles (hand-sewing and quilting betweens), pins (long, thin sharp pins are best), sharp scissors or shears, a thimble, template materials (plastic or cardboard), marking tools (chalk marker, water-erasable pen and a No. 2 pencil are a few) and a quilting frame or hoop. For piecing and/or quilting by machine, add a sewing machine to the list.

Other sewing basics such as a seam ripper, pincushion, measuring tape and an iron are also necessary. For choosing colors or quilting designs for your quilt, or for designing your own quilt, it is helpful to have on hand graph paper, tracing paper, colored pencils or markers and a ruler.

For making strip-pieced quilts, a rotary cutter, mat and specialty rulers are often used. We recommend an ergonomic rotary cutter, a large self-healing mat and several rulers. If you can choose only one size, a 6" x 24" marked in 1/8" or 1/4" increments is recommended.

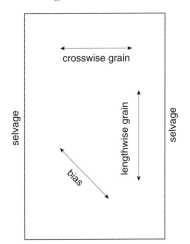

Figure 1
Drawing shows lengthwise, crosswise and bias threads.

Construction Methods

Templates

Traditional Templates. While some quilt instructions in this book use rotary-cut strips and quick sewing methods, a few patterns require templates. Templates are like the pattern pieces used to sew a garment. They are used to cut the fabric pieces which make up the quilt top. There are two types—templates that include a 1/4" seam allowance and those that don't.

Choose the template material and the pattern. Transfer the pattern shapes to the template material with a sharp No. 2 lead pencil. Write the pattern name, piece letter or number, grain line and number to cut for one block or whole quilt on each piece as shown in Figure 3.

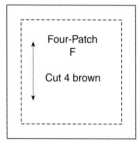

Figure 3
Mark each template with the pattern name and piece identification.

Some patterns require a reversed piece (Figure 4). These patterns are labeled with an R after the piece letter; for example, F and FR. To reverse a template, first cut it with the labeled side up and then with the labeled side down. Compare these to the right and left fronts of a blouse. When making a garment, you accomplish reversed pieces when cutting the pattern on two layers of fabric placed with right sides together. This can be done when cutting templates as well.

If cutting one layer of fabric at a time, first trace the template onto the backside of the fabric with the marked side

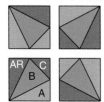

Figure 4
This pattern uses reversed pieces.

down; turn the template over with the marked side up to make reverse pieces.

Appliqué patterns given in this book do not include a seam allowance. Most designs are given in one drawing rather than individual pieces. This saves space while giving you the complete design to trace on the background block to help with placement of the pieces later. Make templates for each shape using the drawing for exact size. Remember to label each piece as for piecing templates.

For hand appliqué, add a seam allowance when cutting pieces from fabric. You may trace the template with label side up on the right side of the fabric if you are careful to mark lightly. The traced line is then the guide for turning the edges under when stitching.

If you prefer to mark on the wrong side of the fabric, turn the template over if you want the pattern to face the same way it does on the page.

For machine appliqué, a seam allowance is not necessary. Trace template onto the right side of the fabric with label facing up. Cut around shape on the traced line.

Piecing

Hand-Piecing Basics. When hand-piecing it is easier to begin with templates which do not include the 1/4" seam allowance. Place the template on the wrong side of the fabric, lining up the marked grain line with lengthwise or crosswise fabric grain. If the piece does not have to be reversed, place with labeled side up. Trace around shape; move, leaving 1/2" between the shapes, and mark again.

When you have marked the appropriate number of pieces, cut out pieces, leaving 1/4" beyond marked line all around each piece.

To piece, refer to assembly drawings to piece units and blocks, if provided. To join two units, place the patches with right sides together. Stick a pin in at the beginning of the seam through both fabric patches, matching the beginning points (Figure 5); for hand-piecing, the seam begins on the traced line, not at the edge of the fabric (see Figure 6).

Figure 5
Stick a pin through fabrics to match the beginning of the seam.

Figure 6
Begin hand-piecing at seam, not at the edge of the fabric. Continue stitching along seam line.

Thread a sharp needle; knot one strand of the thread at the end. Remove the pin and insert the needle in the hole; make a short stitch and then a back-stitch right over the first stitch.

Continue making short stitches with several stitches on the needle at one time. As you stitch, check the back piece often to assure accurate stitching on the seam line. Take a stitch at the end of the seam; backstitch and knot at the same time as shown in Figure 7.

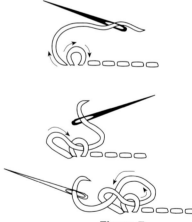

Figure 7
Make a loop in a backstitch to make a knot.

Seams on hand-pieced fabric patches may be finger-pressed toward the darker fabric.

To sew units together, pin fabric patches together, matching seams. Sew as above except where seams meet; at these intersections, backstitch, go through seam to next piece and backstitch again to secure seam joint.

Not all pieced blocks can be stitched with straight seams or in rows. Some patterns require set-in pieces. To begin a set-in seam on a star pattern, pin one side of the square to the proper side of the star point with right sides together, matching corners. Start stitching at the seam line on the outside point; stitch on the marked seam line to the end of the seam line at the center referring to Figure 8.

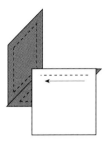

Figure 8
To set a square into a diamond point, match seams and stitch from outside edge to center.

Bring around the adjacent side and pin to the next star point, matching seams. Continue the stitching line from the adjacent seam through corners and to the outside edge of the square as shown in Figure 9.

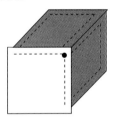

Figure 9
Continue stitching the adjacent side of the square to the next diamond shape in 1 seam from center to outside as shown.

Machine-Piecing. If making templates, include the 1/4" seam allowance on the template for machine-piecing. Place template on the wrong side of the fabric as for hand-piecing except butt pieces against one another when tracing.

Set machine on 2.5 or 12–15 stitches per inch. Join pieces as for hand-piecing for set-in seams; but for other straight seams, begin and end sewing at the end of the fabric patch sewn as shown in Figure 10. No backstitching is necessary when machine-stitching.

Join units as for hand-piecing referring

to the piecing diagrams where needed. Chain piecing (Figure 11—sewing several like units before sewing other units) saves time by eliminating beginning and ending stitches.

When joining machine-pieced units, match seams against each other with seam allowances pressed in opposite directions to reduce bulk and make perfect matching of seams possible (Figure 12).

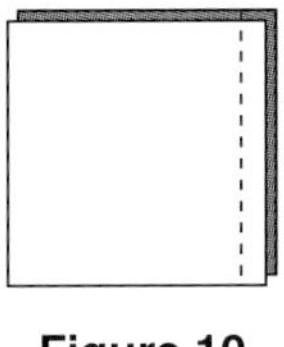

Figure 10
Begin machine-piecing at the end of the piece, not at the end of the seam.

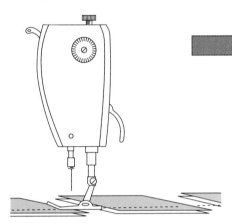

Figure 11
Units may be chain-pieced to save time.

Figure 12
Sew machine-pieced units with seams pressed in opposite directions.

Cutting

Quick-Cutting. Quick-cutting and piecing strips are recommended for making many of the projects in this book. Templates are completely eliminated; instead, a rotary cutter, plastic ruler and mat are used to cut fabric pieces.

When rotary-cutting strips, straighten raw edges of fabric by folding fabric in

fourths across the width as shown in Figure 13. Press down flat; place ruler on fabric square with edge of fabric and make one cut from the folded edge to the outside edge. If strips are not straightened, a wavy strip will result as shown in Figure 14.

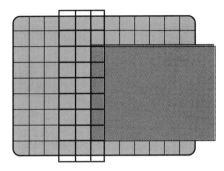

Figure 13
Fold fabric and straighten as shown.

Figure 14
Wavy strips result if fabric is not straightened before cutting.

Always cut away from your body, holding the ruler firmly with the non-cutting hand. Keep fingers away from the edge of the ruler as it is easy for the rotary cutter to slip and jump over the edge of the ruler if cutting is not properly done.

For many strip-pieced blocks two strips are stitched together as shown in Figure 15. The strips are stitched, pressed and cut into segments as shown in Figure 16.

The cut segments are arranged as shown in Figure 17 and stitched to complete, in this example, one Four-Patch block. Although the block shown is very simple, the same methods may be used for more complicated patterns.

The direction to press seams on strip sets is important for accurate piecing later. The normal rule for pressing is to press seams toward the darker fabric to keep the colors from showing through on lighter colors later. For joining segments from strip sets, this rule doesn't always apply.

It is best if seams on adjacent rows are pressed in opposite directions. When aligning segments to stitch rows together, if pressed properly, seam joints will have a seam going in both directions as shown in Figure 18.

If a square is required for the pattern, it can be sub-cut from a strip as shown in Figure 19.

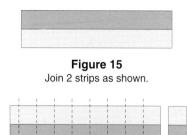

Figure 15
Join 2 strips as shown.

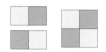

Figure 16
Cut segments from the stitched strip set.

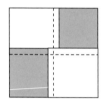

Figure 17
Arrange cut segments to make a Four-Patch block.

Figure 18
Seams go in both directions at seam joints.

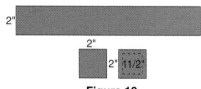

Figure 19
If cutting squares, cut proper-width strip into same-width segments. Here, a 2" strip is cut into 2" segments to create 2" squares. These squares finish at 1 1/2" when sewn.

If you need right triangles with the straight grain on the short sides, you can use the same method, but you need to figure out how wide to cut the strip. Measure the finished size of one short side of the triangle. Add 7/8" to this size for seam allowance. Cut fabric strips this width; cut the strips into the same increment to create squares. Cut the squares on the diagonal to produce triangles. For example, if you need a triangle with a 2" finished height, cut the strips 2 7/8" by the width of the fabric. Cut the strips into 2 7/8" squares. Cut

each square on the diagonal to produce the correct-size triangle with the grain on the short sides (Figure 20).

Triangles sewn together to make squares are called half-square triangles or triangle/squares. When joined, the triangle/square unit has the straight of grain on all outside edges of the block.

Another method of making triangle/squares is shown in Figure 21. Layer two squares with right sides together; draw a diagonal line through the center. Stitch 1/4" on both sides of the line. Cut apart on the drawn line to reveal two stitched triangle/squares.

If you need triangles with the straight of grain on the diagonal, such as for fill-in triangles on the outside edges of a diagonal-set quilt, the procedure is a bit different.

To make these triangles, a square is cut on both diagonals; thus, the straight of grain is on the longest or diagonal side (Figure 22). To figure out the size to cut the square, add 1 1/4" to the needed finished size of the longest side of the

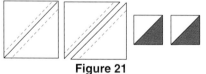

Figure 20
Cut 2" (finished size) triangles from 2 7/8" squares as shown.

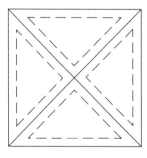

Figure 21
Mark a diagonal line on the square; stitch 1/4" on each side of the line. Cut on line to reveal stitched triangle/squares.

Figure 22
Add 1 1/4" to the finished size of the longest side of the triangle needed and cut on both diagonals to make a quarter-square triangle.

triangle. For example, if you need a triangle with a 12" finished diagonal, cut a 13 1/4" square.

If templates are given, use their measurements to cut fabric strips to correspond with that measurement. The template may be used on the strip to cut pieces quickly. Strip cutting works best for squares, triangles, rectangles and diamonds. Odd-shaped templates are difficult to cut in multiple layers using a rotary cutter.

Foundation Piecing

Foundation Piecing. Paper or fabric foundation pieces are used to make very accurate blocks, provide stability for weak fabrics, and add body and weight to the finished quilt.

Temporary foundation materials include paper, tracing paper, freezer paper and removable interfacing. Permanent foundations include utility fabrics, non-woven interfacing, flannel, fleece and batting.

Methods of marking foundations include basting lines, pencils or pens, needlepunching, tracing wheel, hot-iron transfers, copy machine, premarked, stamps or stencils.

There are two methods of foundation piecing—under-piecing and top-piecing. When under-piecing, the pattern is reversed when tracing. We have not included any patterns for top-piecing. **Note:** *All patterns for which we recommend paper piecing are already reversed in full-size drawings given.*

To under-piece, place a scrap of fabric larger than the lined space on the unlined side of the paper in the No. 1 position. Place piece 2 right sides together with piece 1; pin on seam line, and fold back to check that the piece will cover space 2 before stitching.

Tips & Techniques
If you cannot see the lines on the backside of the paper when paper-piecing, draw over lines with a small felt-tip marker. The lines should now be visible on the backside to help with placement of fabric pieces.

Stitch along line on the lined side of the paper—fabric will not be visible. Sew several stitches beyond the beginning and ending of the line. Backstitching is not required as another fabric seam will cover this seam.

Remove pin; finger-press piece 2 flat. Continue adding all pieces in numerical order in the same manner until all pieces are stitched to paper. Trim excess to outside line (1/4" larger all around than finished size of the block).

Tracing paper can be used as a temporary foundation. It is removed when blocks are complete and stitched together. To paper-piece, copy patterns given here using a copy machine or trace each block individually. Measure the finished paper foundations to insure accuracy in copying.

Appliqué

Appliqué. Appliqué is the process of applying one piece of fabric on top of another for decorative or functional purposes.

Making Templates. Most appliqué designs given here are shown as full-size drawings for the completed designs. The drawings show dotted lines to indicate where one piece overlaps another. Other marks indicate placement of embroidery stitches for decorative purposes such as eyes, lips, flowers, etc.

For hand appliqué, trace each template onto the right side of the fabric with template right side up. Cut around shape, adding a 1/8"–1/4" seam allowance.

Before the actual appliqué process begins, cut the background block and prepare it for stitching. Most appliqué designs are centered on the block. To find the center of the background square, fold it in half and in half again; crease with your fingers. Now unfold

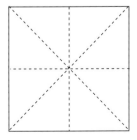

Figure 23
Fold background to mark centers as shown.

and fold diagonally and crease; repeat for other corners referring to Figure 23. Center-line creases to help position the design. If centering the appliqué design is important, an X has been placed on each drawing to mark the center of the design. Match the X with the creased center of the background block when placing pieces.

If you have a full-size drawing of the design, as is given with most appliqué designs in this book, it might help you to draw on the background block to help with placement. Transfer the design to a large piece of tracing paper. Place the paper on top of the design; use masking tape to hold in place. Trace design onto paper.

If you don't have a light box, tape the pattern on a window; center the background block on top and tape in place. Trace the design onto the background block with a water-erasable marker or chalk pencil. This drawing will mark exactly where the fabric pieces should be placed on the background block.

Hand Appliqué. Traditional hand appliqué uses a template made from the desired finished shape without seam allowance added.

After fabric is prepared, trace the desired shape onto the right side of the fabric with a water-erasable marker, light lead or chalk pencil. Leave at least 1/2" between design motifs when tracing to allow for the seam allowance when cutting out the shapes.

When the desired number of shapes needed has been drawn on the fabric pieces, cut out shapes leaving 1/8"–1/4" all around drawn line for turning under.

Turn the shape's edges over on the drawn or stitched line. When turning the edges under, make sharp corners sharp and smooth edges smooth. The fabric patch should retain the shape of the template used to cut it.

Figure 24
Concave curves should be clipped before turning as shown.

When turning in concave curves, clip to seams and baste the seam allowance over as shown in Figure 24.

During the actual appliqué process, you may be layering one shape on top of another. Where two fabrics overlap, the underneath piece does not have to be turned under or stitched down.

If possible, trim away the underneath fabric when the block is finished by carefully cutting away the background from underneath and then cutting away unnecessary layers to reduce bulk and avoid shadows from darker fabrics showing through on light fabrics.

For hand appliqué, position the fabric shapes on the background block and pin or baste them in place. Using a blind stitch or appliqué stitch, sew pieces in place with matching thread and small stitches. Start with background pieces first and work up to foreground pieces. Appliqué the pieces in place on the background in numerical order, if given, layering as necessary.

Machine Appliqué. There are several products available to help make the machine-appliqué process easier and faster.

Fusible transfer web is a commercial product similar to iron-on interfacings except it has two sticky sides. It is used to adhere appliqué shapes to the background with heat. Paper is adhered to one side of the web.

To use, dry-iron the sticky side of the fusible product onto the wrong side of the chosen fabric. Draw desired shapes onto the paper and cut them out. Peel off the paper and dry-iron the shapes in place on the background fabric. The shape will stay in place while you stitch around it. This process adds a little bulk or stiffness to the appliquéd shape and makes hand quilting through the layers difficult.

For successful machine appliqué a tear-off stabilizer is recommended. This product is placed under the background fabric while machine appliqué is being done. It is torn away when the work is finished. This kind of stabilizer keeps the background fabric from pulling during the machine-appliqué process.

During the actual machine-appliqué process, you will be layering one shape on top of another. Where two fabrics overlap, the underneath piece does not have to be turned under or stitched down.

Thread the top of the machine with thread to match the fabric patches or with threads that coordinate or contrast with fabrics. Rayon thread is a good choice when a sheen is desired on the finished appliqué stitches. Do not use rayon thread in the bobbin; use all-purpose thread.

Set your machine to make a zigzag stitch and practice on scraps of similar weight to check the tension. If you can see the bobbin thread on the top of the appliqué, adjust your machine to make a balanced stitch. Different-width stitches are available; choose one that will not overpower the appliqué shapes. In some cases these appliqué stitches will be used as decorative stitches as well and you may want the thread to show.

If using a stabilizer, place this under the background fabric and pin or fuse in place. Place shapes as for hand-appliqué and stitch all around shapes by machine.

When all machine work is complete, remove stabilizer from the back referring to the manufacturer's instructions.

Tips & Techniques

Before machine-piecing fabric patches together, test your sewing machine for positioning an accurate 1/4" seam allowance. There are several tools to help guarantee this. Some machine needles may be moved to allow the presser-foot edge to be a 1/4" guide.

A special foot may be purchased for your machine that will guarantee an accurate 1/4" seam. A piece of masking tape can be placed on the throat plate of your sewing machine to mark the 1/4" seam. A plastic stick-on ruler may be used instead of tape with the same results.

Putting It All Together

Many steps are required to prepare a quilt top for quilting, including setting the blocks together, adding borders, choosing and marking quilting designs, layering the top, batting and backing for quilting, quilting or tying the layers and finishing the edges of the quilt.

As you begin the process of finishing your quilt top, strive for a neat, flat quilt with square sides and corners, not for perfection—that will come with time and practice.

Finishing the Top

Settings. Most quilts are made by sewing individual blocks together in rows which, when joined, create a design. There are several other methods used to join blocks. Sometimes the setting choice is determined by the block's design. For example, a house block should be placed upright on a quilt, not sideways or upside down.

Plain blocks can be alternated with pieced or appliquéd blocks in a straight set. Making a quilt using plain blocks saves time; half the number of pieced or appliquéd blocks are needed to make the same-size quilt as shown in Figure 1.

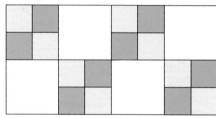

Figure 1
Alternate plain blocks with pieced blocks to save time.

Adding Borders. Borders are an integral part of the quilt and should complement the colors and designs used in the quilt center. Borders frame a quilt just like a mat and frame do a picture.

If fabric strips are added for borders, they may be mitered or butted at the corners as shown in Figures 2 and 3.

To determine the size for butted-border strips, measure across the center of the completed quilt top from one side raw edge to the other side raw edge. This measurement will include a 1/4" seam allowance. Cut two border strips that length by the chosen width of the

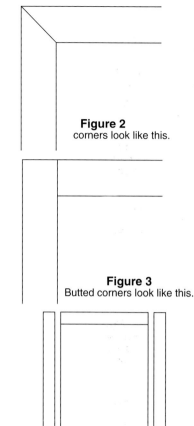

Figure 2
corners look like this.

Figure 3
Butted corners look like this.

Figure 4
Sew border strips to opposite sides; sew remaining 2 strips to remaining sides to make butted corners.

border. Sew these strips to the top and bottom of the pieced center referring to Figure 4. Press the seam allowance toward the border strips.

Measure across the completed quilt top at the center, from top raw edge to bottom raw edge, including the two border strips already added. Cut two border strips that length by the chosen width of the border. Sew a strip to each of the two remaining sides as shown in Figure 4. Press the seams toward the border strips.

To make mitered corners, measure the quilt as before. To this add twice the width of the border and 1/2" for seam allowances to determine the length of the strips. Repeat for opposite sides. Center and sew on each strip, stopping stitching 1/4" from corner, leaving the remainder of the strip dangling.

Press corners at a 45-degree angle to form a crease. Stitch from the inside quilt corner to the outside on the creased line. Trim excess away after stitching and press mitered seams open (Figures 5–7).

Carefully press the entire quilt top. Avoid pulling and stretching while pressing, which would distort shapes.

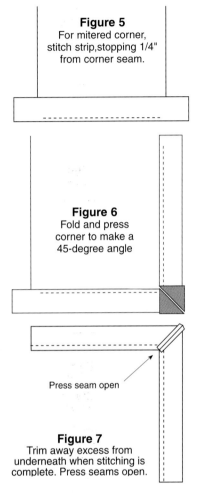

Figure 5
For mitered corner, stitch strip, stopping 1/4" from corner seam.

Figure 6
Fold and press corner to make a 45-degree angle

Press seam open

Figure 7
Trim away excess from underneath when stitching is complete. Press seams open.

Getting Ready to Quilt

Choosing a Quilting Design. If you choose to hand- or machine-quilt your finished top, you will need to choose a design for quilting.

There are several types of quilting designs, some of which may not have to be marked. The easiest of the unmarked designs is in-the-ditch quilting. Here the quilting stitches are placed in the valley created by the seams joining two pieces together or next to the edge of an appliqué design. There is no need to mark a top for in-the-ditch quilting. Machine quilters choose this option because the stitches are not as obvious on the finished quilt (Figure 8).

Outline-quilting 1/4" or more away from seams or appliqué shapes is anoth-

er no-mark alternative (Figure 9) which prevents having to sew through the layers made by seams, thus making stitching easier.

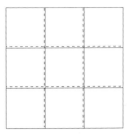

Figure 8
In-the-ditch quilting is done in the seam that joins 2 pieces.

Figure 9
Outline-quilting 1/4" away from seam is a popular choice for quilting.

If you are not comfortable eyeballing the 1/4" (or other distance), masking tape is available in different widths and is helpful to place on straight-edge designs to mark the quilting line. If using masking tape, place the tape right up against the seam and quilt close to the other edge.

Meander or free-motion quilting by machine fills in open spaces and doesn't require marking. It is fun and easy to stitch as shown in Figure 10.

Figure 10
Machine meander quilting fills in large spaces.

Marking the Top for Quilting or Tying. If you choose a fancy or allover design for quilting, you will need to transfer the design to your quilt top before layering with the backing and

batting. You may use a sharp medium-lead or silver pencil on light background fabrics. Test the pencil marks to guarantee that they will wash out of your quilt top when quilting is complete; or be sure your quilting stitches cover the pencil marks. Mechanical pencils with very fine points may be used successfully to mark quilts.

Manufactured quilt-design templates are available in many designs and sizes and are cut out of a durable plastic template material which is easy to use.

To make a permanent quilt-design template, choose a template material on which to transfer the design. See-through plastic is the best as it will let you place the design while allowing you to see where it is in relation to your quilt design without moving it. Place the design on the quilt top where you want it and trace around it with your marking tool. Pick up the quilting template and place again; repeat marking.

No matter what marking method you use, remember—the marked lines should *never show* on the finished quilt. When the top is marked, it is ready for layering.

Preparing the Quilt Backing. The quilt backing is a very important feature of your quilt. In most cases, the materials list for each quilt in this book gives the size requirements for the backing, not the yardage needed. Exceptions to this are when the backing fabric is also used on the quilt top and yardage is given for that fabric.

A backing is generally cut at least 4" larger than the quilt top or 2" larger on all sides. For a 64" x 78" finished quilt, the backing would need to be at least 68" x 82".

To avoid having the seam across the center of the quilt backing, cut or tear

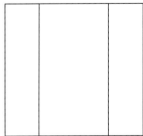

Figure 11
Center 1 backing piece with a piece on each side.

one of the right-length pieces in half and sew half to each side of the second piece as shown in Figure 11.

Quilts that need backing more than 88" wide may be pieced in horizontal pieces as shown in Figure 12.

Figure 12
Horizontal seams may be used on backing pieces.

Layering the Quilt Sandwich.
Layering the quilt top with the batting and backing is time-consuming. Open the batting several days before you need it and place over a bed or flat on the floor to help flatten the creases caused from its being folded up in the bag for so long.

Iron the backing piece, folding in half both vertically and horizontally and pressing to mark centers.

If you will not be quilting on a frame, place the backing right side down on a clean floor or table. Start in the center and push any wrinkles or bunches flat. Use masking tape to tape the edges to the floor or large clips to hold the backing to the edges of the table. The backing should be taut.

Place the batting on top of the backing, matching centers using fold lines as guides; flatten out any wrinkles. Trim the batting to the same size as the backing.

Fold the quilt top in half lengthwise and place on top of the batting, wrong side against the batting, matching centers. Unfold quilt and, working from the center to the outside edges, smooth out any wrinkles or lumps.

To hold the quilt layers together for quilting, baste by hand or use safety pins. If basting by hand, thread a long thin needle with a long piece of unknotted white or off-white thread. Starting

in the center and leaving a long tail, make 4"–6" stitches toward the outside edge of the quilt top, smoothing as you baste. Start at the center again and work toward the outside as shown in Figure 13.

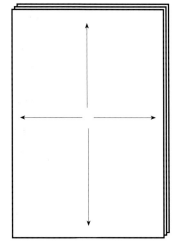

Figure 13
Baste from the center to the outside edges.

If quilting by machine, you may prefer to use safety pins for holding your quilt sandwich together. Start in the center of the quilt and pin to the outside, leaving pins open until all are placed. When you are satisfied that all layers are smooth, close the pins.

Quilting

Hand Quilting. Hand quilting is the process of placing stitches through the quilt top, batting and backing to hold them together. While it is a functional process, it also adds beauty and loft to the finished quilt.

To begin, thread a sharp between needle with an 18" piece of quilting thread. Tie a small knot in the end of the thread. Position the needle about 1/2" to 1" away from the starting point on quilt top. Sink the needle through the top into the batting layer but not through the backing. Pull the needle up at the starting point of the quilting design. Pull the needle and thread until the knot

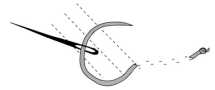

Figure 14
Start the needle through the top layer of fabric 1/2"–1" away from quilting line with knot on top of fabric.

sinks through the top into the batting (Figure 14).

Some stitchers like to take a backstitch at the beginning while others prefer to begin the first stitch here. Take small, even running stitches along the marked quilting line (Figure 15). Keep one hand positioned underneath to feel the needle go all the way through to the backing.

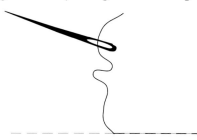

Figure 15
Make small, even running stitches on marked quilting line.

Tips & Techniques
Knots should not show on the quilt top or back. Learn to sink the knot into the batting at the beginning and ending of the quilting thread for successful stitches.

When you have nearly run out of thread, wind the thread around the needle several times to make a small knot and pull it close to the fabric. Insert the needle into the fabric on the quilting line and come out with the needle 1/2" to 1" away, pulling the knot into the fabric layers the same as when you started. Pull and cut thread close to fabric. The end should disappear inside after cutting. Some quilters prefer to take a backstitch with a loop through it for a knot to end.

Making 12–18 stitches per inch is a nice goal, but a more realistic goal is seven to nine stitches per inch. If you cannot accomplish this right away, strive for even stitches—all the same size—that look as good on the back as on the front.

You will perfect your quilting stitches as you gain experience, your stitches will get better with each project and your style will be uniquely your own.

Machine Quilting. Successful machine quilting requires practice and a good relationship with your sewing machine.

Prepare the quilt for machine quilting in the same way as for hand quilting. Use safety pins to hold the layers together instead of basting with thread.

Presser-foot quilting is best used for straight-line quilting because the presser bar lever does not need to be continually lifted.

Set the machine on a longer stitch length (three or eight to 10 stitches to the inch). Too tight a stitch causes puckering and fabric tucks, either on the quilt top or backing. An even-feed or walking foot helps to eliminate the tucks and puckering by feeding the upper and lower layers through the machine evenly. Before you begin, loosen the amount of pressure on the presser foot.

Special machine-quilting needles work best to penetrate the three layers in your quilt.

Decide on a design. Quilting in the ditch is not quite as visible, but if you quilt with the feed dogs engaged, it means turning the quilt frequently. It is not easy to fit a rolled-up quilt through the small opening on the sewing machine head.

Meander quilting is the easiest way to machine-quilt—and it is fun. Meander

quilting is done using an appliqué or darning foot with the feed dogs dropped. It is sort of like scribbling. Simply move the quilt top around under the foot and make stitches in a random pattern to fill the space. The same method may be used to outline a quilt design. The trick is the same as in hand-quilting; you are striving for stitches of uniform size. Your hands are in complete control of the design.

If machine-quilting is of interest to you, there are several very good books available at quilt shops that will help you become a successful machine quilter.

Tied Quilts, or Comforters. Would you rather tie your quilt layers together than quilt them? Tied quilts are often referred to as comforters. The advantage of tying is that it takes so much less time and the required skills can be learned quickly.

If a top will be tied, choose a thick, bonded batting—one that will not separate during washing. For tying, use pearl cotton, embroidery floss, or strong yarn in colors that match or coordinate with the fabrics in your quilt top.

Decide on a pattern for tying. Many quilts are tied at the corners and centers of the blocks and at sashing joints. Try to tie every 4"–6". Special designs can be used for tying, but most quilts are tied in conventional ways. Begin tying in the center and work to the outside edges.

To make the tie, thread a large needle with a long thread (yarn, floss or crochet cotton); do not knot. Push the needle through the quilt top to the back, leaving a 3"–4" length on top. Move the needle to the next position without cutting thread. Take another stitch through the layers; repeat until thread is almost used up.

Cut thread between stitches, leaving an equal amount of thread on each stitch. Tie a knot with the two thread ends.

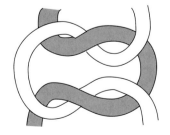

Figure 16
Make a square knot as shown.

Tie again to make a square knot referring to Figure 16. Trim thread ends to desired length.

Finishing the Edges

After your quilt is tied or quilted, the edges need to be finished. Decide how you want the edges of your quilt finished before layering the backing and batting with the quilt top.

Without Binding—Self-Finish. There is one way to eliminate adding an edge finish. This is done before quilting. Place the batting on a flat surface. Place the pieced top right side up on the batting. Place the backing right sides together with the pieced top. Pin and/or baste the layers together to hold flat referring to page 171.

Begin stitching in the center of one side using a 1/4" seam allowance, reversing at the beginning and end of the seam. Continue stitching all around and back to the beginning side. Leave a 12" or larger opening. Clip corners to reduce excess. Turn right side out through the opening. Slipstitch the opening closed by hand. The quilt may now be quilted by hand or machine.

The disadvantage to this method is that once the edges are sewn in, any creases or wrinkles that might form during the quilting process cannot be flattened out. Tying is the preferred method for finishing a quilt constructed using this method.

Bringing the backing fabric to the front is another way to finish the quilt's edge without binding. To accomplish this, complete the quilt as for hand or machine quilting. Trim the batting *only* even with the front. Trim the backing 1" larger than the completed top all around.

Turn the backing edge in 1/2" and then turn over to the front along edge of batting. The folded edge may be machine-stitched close to the edge through all layers, or blind-stitched in place to finish.

The front may be turned to the back. If using this method, a wider front border is needed. The backing and batting are trimmed 1" *smaller* than the top and the top edge is turned under 1/2" and then turned to the back and stitched in place.

One more method of self-finish may be used. The top and backing may be stitched together by hand at the edge. To accomplish this, all quilting must be stopped 1/2" from the quilt-top edge. The top and backing of the quilt are trimmed even and the batting is trimmed to 1/4"–1/2" smaller. The edges of the top and backing are turned in 1/4"–1/2" and blind-stitched together at the very edge.

These methods do not require the use of extra fabric and save time in preparation of binding strips; they are not as durable as an added binding.

Binding. The technique of adding extra fabric at the edges of the quilt is called binding. The binding encloses the edges and adds an extra layer of fabric for durability.

To prepare the quilt for the addition of the binding, trim the batting and backing layers flush with the top of the quilt using a rotary cutter and ruler or shears. Using a walking-foot attachment (sometimes called an even-feed foot attachment), machine-baste the three layers together all around approximately 1/8" from the cut edge.

The list of materials given with each quilt in this book often includes a number of yards of self-made or purchased binding. Bias binding may be purchased in packages and in many colors. The advantage to self-made binding is that you can use fabrics from your quilt to coordinate colors.

Double-fold, straight-grain binding and double-fold, bias-grain binding are two of the most commonly used types of binding.

Double-fold, straight-grain binding is used on smaller projects with right-angle corners. Double-fold, bias-grain binding is best suited for bed-size quilts or quilts with rounded corners.

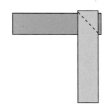

Figure 17
Join binding strips in a diagonal seam to eliminate bulk as shown.

To make double-fold, straight-grain binding, cut 2"-wide strips of fabric across the width or down the length of the fabric totaling the perimeter of the quilt plus 10". The strips are joined as shown in Figure 17 and pressed in half wrong sides together along the length using an iron on a cotton setting with *no* steam.

Lining up the raw edges, place the binding on the top of the quilt and begin sewing (again using the walking foot) approximately 6" from the beginning of the binding strip. Stop sewing 1/4" from the first corner, leave the needle in the quilt, turn and sew diagonally to the corner as shown in Figure 18.

Fold the binding at a 45-degree angle up and away from the quilt as shown in Figure 19 and back down flush with the raw edges. Starting at the top raw edge of the quilt, begin sewing the next side as shown in Figure 20. Repeat at the next three corners.

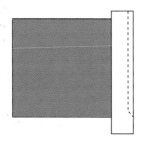

Figure 18
Sew to within 1/4" of corner; leave needle in quilt, turn and stitch diagonally off the corner of the quilt.

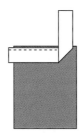

Figure 19
Fold binding at a 45-degree angle up and away from quilt as shown.

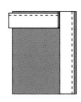

Figure 20
Fold the binding strips back down, flush with the raw edge, and begin sewing.

As you approach the beginning of the binding strip, stop stitching and overlap the binding 1/2" from the edge; trim. Join the two ends with a 1/4" seam allowance and press the seam open. Reposition the joined binding along the

edge of the quilt and resume stitching to the beginning.

To finish, bring the folded edge of the binding over the raw edges and blind-stitch the binding in place over the machine-stitching line on the backside. Hand-miter the corners on the back as shown in Figure 21.

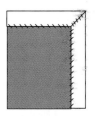

Figure 21
Miter and stitch the corners as shown.

If you are making a quilt to be used on a bed, you will want to use double-fold, bias-grain bindings because the many threads that cross each other along the fold at the edge of the quilt make it a more durable binding.

Cut 2"-wide bias strips from a large square of fabric. Join the strips as illustrated in Figure 17 and press the seams open. Fold the beginning end of the bias strip 1/4" from the raw edge and press. Fold the joined strips in half along the long side, wrong sides together, and press with *no* steam (Figure 22).

Figure 22
Fold end in and press strip in half.

Follow the same procedures as previously described for preparing the quilt top and sewing the binding to the quilt top. Treat the corners just as you treated

Figure 23
Round corners to eliminate square-corner finishes.

them with straight-grain binding.

Since you are using bias-grain binding, you do have the option to just eliminate the corners if this option doesn't interfere with the patchwork in the quilt. Round the corners off by placing one of your dinner plates at the corner and rotary-cutting the gentle curve (Figure 23).

Figure 23
Round corners to eliminate square-corner finishes.

As you approach the beginning of the binding strip, stop stitching and lay the end across the beginning so it will slip inside the fold. Cut the end at a 45-degree angle so the raw edges are contained inside the beginning of the strip (Figure 24). Resume stitching to the beginning. Bring the fold to the back of the quilt and hand-stitch as previously described.

Figure 24
End the binding strips as shown.

Overlapped corners are not quite as easy as rounded ones, but a bit easier than mitering. To make overlapped corners, sew binding strips to opposite sides of the quilt top. Stitch edges down to finish. Trim ends even.

Sew a strip to each remaining side, leaving 1 1/2"–2" excess at each end. Turn quilt over and fold binding down even with previous finished edge as shown in Figure 25.

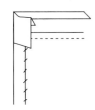

Figure 25
Fold end of binding even with previous edge.

Fold binding in toward quilt and stitch down as before, enclosing the previous bound edge in the seam as shown in Figure 26. It may be necessary to trim the folded-down section to reduce bulk.

Figure 26
An overlapped corner is not quite as neat as a mitered corner.

Making Continuous Bias Binding

Instead of cutting individual bias strips and sewing them together, you may make continuous bias binding.

Cut a square 18" x 18" from chosen binding fabric. Cut the square once on the diagonal to make two triangles as shown in Figure 27. With right sides together, sew the two triangles together with a 1/4" seam allowance as shown in Figure 28; press seam open to reduce bulk.

Mark lines every 2 1/4" on the wrong side of the fabric as shown in Figure 29. Bring the short ends together, right sides together, offsetting one line as shown in Figure 30 to make a tube; stitch. This will seem awkward.

Begin cutting at point A as shown in Figure 31; continue cutting along

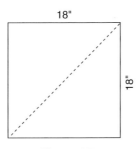

18"

18"

Figure 27
Cut 18" square on the diagonal.

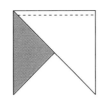

Figure 28
Sew the triangles together.

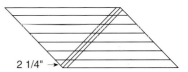

2 1/4"

Figure 29
Mark lines every 2 1/4".

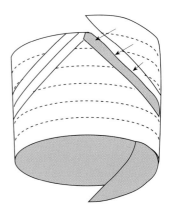

Figure 30
Sew short ends together, offsetting lines to make a tube.

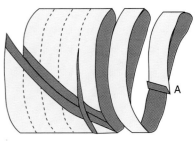

A

Figure 31
Cut along marked lines, starting at A.

marked line to make one continuous strip. Fold strip in half along length with wrong sides together; press. Sew to quilt edges as instructed previously for bias binding.

Final Touches

If your quilt will be hung on the wall, a hanging sleeve is required. Other options include purchased plastic rings or fabric tabs. The best choice is a fabric sleeve, which will evenly distribute the weight of the quilt across the top edge, rather than at selected spots where tabs or rings are stitched, keep the quilt hanging straight and not damage the batting.

To make a sleeve, measure across the top of the finished quilt. Cut an 8"-wide piece of muslin equal to that length—you may need to seam several muslin strips together to make the required length.

Fold in 1/4" on each end of the muslin strip and press. Fold again and stitch to hold. Fold the muslin strip lengthwise with right sides together. Sew along the long side to make a tube. Turn the tube right side out; press with seam at bottom or centered on the back.

Hand-stitch the tube along the top of the quilt and the bottom of the tube to the quilt back making sure the quilt lies flat. Stitches should not go through to the front of the quilt and don't need to be too close together as shown in Figure 32.

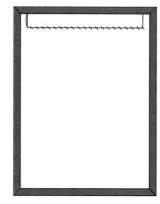

Figure 32
Sew a sleeve to the top
back of the quilt.

Slip a wooden dowel or long curtain rod through the sleeve to hang.

When the quilt is finally complete, it should be signed and dated. Use a permanent pen on the back of the quilt. Other methods include cross-stitching your name and date on the front or back or making a permanent label which may be stitched to the back.

Special Thanks

We would like to thank the talented quilt designers whose work is featured in this collection.

Fabrics & Supplies

Page 49: Patched Cathedral Window—Coats & Clark Dual Duty thread and Embroidery/Crewel size 8 needle, Olfa rotary cutter, Omnigrid ruler and Omnimat by Omnigrid

Page 109: Tied Up for Christmas—Pellon Stitch-n-Tear fabric stabilizer and Wonder-Under fusible transfer web, Sulky gold metallic embroidery thread

Page 126: Christmas Star—Master Piece 45 ruler and Static Stickers

Page 129: Poinsettias—Master Piece 45 ruler and Static Stickers

Page 159: Fiesta Stars—RJR fabrics, Warm & Natural cotton batting, Sulky Tear Easy stabilizer, Sew/Fit tools